Marta Poblet · Pompeu Casanovas ·
Víctor Rodríguez-Doncel

Linked Democracy

Foundations, Tools, and Applications

Marta Poblet
Graduate School of Business and Law
RMIT University
Melbourne, VIC, Australia

Víctor Rodríguez-Doncel
Ontology Engineering Group
Polytechnic University of Madrid (UPM)
Madrid, Spain

Pompeu Casanovas
La Trobe Law School
La Trobe University
Bundoora, Melbourne, VIC, Australia

UAB Institute of Law and Technology
(IDT-UAB)
Universitat Autònoma de Barcelona
Barcelona, Spain

https://doi.org/10.1007/978-3-030-13363-4

Preface

It is only by mobilizing knowledge that is widely dispersed across a genuinely diverse community that a free society can hope to outperform its rivals while remaining true to its values.

(Ober 2008, 5)

The technologies of the twenty-first century are bringing to reality the dream of a fully connected planet. Computers, algorithms and the Internet of Things (IoT) augment exponentially our capacity to link people, data and systems as never before in history. Mobile devices, server farms and grids increase their computing power by orders of magnitude to process staggering masses of data. Refined heuristics profile our actions, predict our needs and read the source code of our thoughts. Our fridges, stoves and toasters will be soon talking to each other with no humans in the loop. Will they also conspire against us, as in a post-Orwellian IoT farm?

The age of connectedness brings an unprecedented promise of exceptionally distributed data, information and knowledge. Yet, the dystopian nightmare of a metadata hydra emerging from our data lakes is also looming. Our human–computer interactions, like Schrödinger cats in sealed boxes, are a blur of possibilities (so we better try hard to not end up like the cats!).

This book, the reader may rest assured, unveils no new paradigm on quantum democracy. Nevertheless, there is a bit of a thought experiment in these pages, and it stems from combining our different backgrounds as researchers working in the areas of computer science, political science, law and philosophy. So, this is the experiment we suggest: If all data, information and knowledge that is currently contained in digital silos were searchable, linkable and shareable, what benefits would this bring for democracy? What if we applied the principles of Linked Open Data to the emergent institutions of the digital democracy ecosystem so that, as Ober suggests, distributed knowledge could be effectively mobilised and we remained free societies true to our values? Which meta-rules would this new scenario require? Would we need a new meta-rule of law?

These are the theoretical questions guiding the chapters of this book. But our proposal is also deeply anchored in our own experiences with some emergent practices where collective intelligence emerges from connecting people, technology and data. These experiences are also practically simultaneous in time. In late 2010, Marta Poblet joined a newly formed group of volunteers providing online support to emergency and disaster management organisations in disaster response. The Standby Task Force (SBTF) was then a loosely connected group of individuals across the world who would scramble at the request of help from formal organisations. A few volunteers would act as coordinators of teams that volunteers could join to perform different tasks: social media monitoring, geolocation of events, verification of reports and analysis. These tasks could be structured, shared and visualised using Ushahidi, an open-source, crowdsourcing platform built in Kenya by activists and software developers following the presidential election of 2007. SBTF volunteers developed protocols and workflows as they deployed in the aftermath of floods (Pakistan 2011, Colombia 2012), typhoons (Yolanda 2012, Pablo 2013), earthquakes (Nepal 2015), humanitarian crisis (Libya 2011, Balkans 2015) and elections (Kenya 2012). They also coordinated their tasks through online platforms such as Skype, Ning or, more recently, Slack. This data-intense, largely distributed effort led to the emergence of collective intelligence about crises, affected populations, and on how to leverage online, remote help for the offline, local response. Digital maps are the outputs of both distributed tasks and collective intelligence (as related datasets and situation reports are), but traces of that emerging collective intelligence were also visible in chats, Google Docs, protocols and workflows. Question about how to properly manage, archive and reuse collective intelligence and its digital outputs was already raised in 2010 for emergency and disaster management. We now raise them for democracy.

Pompeu Casanovas is a Law & Technology and Law & Society scholar. Since 2003, he has been involved in the initial development of the Semantic Web in many national and EU projects on information systems, judicial institutions and new regulatory frameworks. From that standpoint, he has witnessed the emergence of relational forms of law and the growing importance of dialogue, interactions and the social fabric in institutional settings and institutional design. From 2008 to 2011, he served as scientific director of the Catalan White Book on Mediation, a collective endeavour of sixteen research teams and more than one hundred researchers. Catalonia's population had grown from 6 to 7.5 million inhabitants in ten years due to intense migration flows. All public services—from schools to care units and hospitals—had to grapple with the challenges of this rapid influx. Much to everyone's surprise, the findings showed that those challenges had been handled in the first place by ordinary people in neighbourhoods and towns, as well as by the professionals in the public sector (teachers, doctors, nurses, administrator, etc.), rather than led by the government or its public policies. As of 2008, 2% of the Catalan population had participated in mediation processes, and 10% in social support activities. He learnt that law, policies and regulations matter, but democratic culture ranks first.

Víctor Rodríguez-Doncel is a computer scientist who has witnessed the emergence of machine-readable licences in the Web of Data. When the first Creative Commons licences were released in December 2002, few would have believed they would reach the popularity they have now. Up to 2018, over 1.4 billion works have been published along with a Creative Commons licence, unleashing a formidable amount of creativity and knowledge available to anyone. In a more silent revolution, licences and other sorts of agreements are now being translated into their equivalent digital counterparts, designed for computers to reason with. Víctor has edited international standards to represent machine-readable contracts (ISO/IEC 21000-20), computer policies (W3C ODRL) and the content value chain (ISO/IEC 21000-19), always using Semantic Web technologies. He believes that if the culture of sharing is supported by intelligent technologies, a new breed of resources will be available to anyone and the almighty Artificial Intelligence algorithms crunching data will not remain a weapon available only to the few. For its intrinsic nature, the Semantic Web is the key tool towards building a global network of distributed data, knowledge and decision power.

Marta, Víctor and Pompeu have been collaborating for a long time in a number of research projects and publications. This book draws from this previous work to bring recent advances in the Web of Data to democratic theory and law. We believe that the opportunities and challenges of building infrastructures for Linked Data—a term coined by Tim Berners-Lee in 2006—can be of interest to political scientists and legal scholars. Data, information and knowledge that can be freely accessed, shared and reused amplify our resources and capacities as citizens in modern democracies. This may even help us to reconsider concepts such as 'expertise', 'participation' or 'governance' under a new light. This book is just one step in that direction.

Melbourne, Australia — Marta Poblet
Melbourne, Australia — Pompeu Casanovas
Madrid, Spain — Víctor Rodríguez-Doncel

Acknowledgements

In Chaps. 1–5

Law and Policy Program of the Australian Government-funded Data to Decisions Cooperative Research Centre (http://www.d2dcrc.com.au/); Crowdsourcing DER2012-39492-C02-01; Meta-Rule of Law DER2016-78108-P, Research of Excellence, Spain; LYNX, Building the Legal Knowledge Graph for Smart Compliance Services in Multilingual Europe, EU H2020 780602; SPIRIT, Scalable privacy preserving intelligence analysis for resolving identities. EU H2020, 786993.

Figures in Chap. 4

'Network' by Brennan Novak; 'Folder' by Jivan; 'Hexagons' by CreativeStall; 'Scale tool' by Oliviou Stoian; 'Recycle' by BomSymbols; 'Archive update' by Bernar Novalyi; Frame by Magicon; Settings adjustments by Naim.

Contents

List of Figures

List of Tables

Chapter 1
Introduction to Linked Data

Abstract This chapter presents Linked Data, a new form of distributed data on the web which is especially suitable to be manipulated by machines and to share knowledge. By adopting the linked data publication paradigm, anybody can publish data on the web, relate it to data resources published by others and run artificial intelligence algorithms in a smooth manner. Open linked data resources may democratize the future access to knowledge by the mass of internet users, either directly or mediated through algorithms. Governments have enthusiastically adopted these ideas, which is in harmony with the broader open data movement.

Keywords Linked data · Semantic web · Democracy · Ontologies · Knowledge representation · eDemocracy

1.1 Introduction

More than half of the world's population has access to the Internet. Vast amounts of knowledge accumulated in roughly 2 billion websites are available to anyone who is able to read and can afford an internet connection.

Entertainment habits, interpersonal human relations and almost any conceivable aspect of human life have been profoundly transformed with the arrival of the internet. Yet modern democracies have remained relatively unaffected. It is true that propaganda techniques have undergone changes, political parties organize their campaign strategies differently and the idea of eDemocracy is perhaps about to hatch; but the public institutions, the habits of citizens and the overall political game are all apparently the same.

We have to indulge—Internet is a new thing. But a careful observation of the evolution of technologies and the new organizational forms they enable reveal discrete signs of change, now with little effect but potentially of much impact.

This chapter introduces some new technologies and ideas which may seem irrelevant today, but which will probably exert a powerful influence on the forthcoming transformations of the concept of democracy.

M. Poblet et al., *Linked Democracy*, SpringerBriefs in Law,
https://doi.org/10.1007/978-3-030-13363-4_1

1.2 The World Wide Web as a Source of Data and Knowledge

1.2.1 Data, Information and Knowledge

Marshall McLuhan described technology as extensions of man (McLuhan 1964), whereby our bodies and our senses are extended beyond their natural limits. Certainly, a shovel is an improvement of our hands when we dig a trench and telescopes are augmented eyes when we look at the stars. In top level chess tournaments, chess players prepare their games and study their opponents with a joint team of humans and machine—machines also extend human's capabilities for thinking.

In order to make a value judgement, we need data—this is a truism. But today we also need machines which need data. Whenever we take an important decision, we usually google for some related information. Our decisions are mediated by information provided by a company, or a handful of companies, whose interests may not match our interests. Maybe in the future we will have a wider range of algorithms to apply to a common pool of open knowledge—both data and algorithms are essential extensions of our mind enhancing and rational processes.

This book is about linked democracy, a concept of democracy where knowledge plays a central role; and this relation between data, algorithms and knowledge has to be studied in more detail. One of the possible conceptual frameworks is the popular pyramid of data, information and knowledge, represented in Fig. 1.1 in a manner that suggests that data is abundant, information not so much and knowledge is scarce.

We can simply define *data* as 'the symbols on which operations can be performed by a calculator, either human or machine'. Data conveys information about any conceivable entity—the stars, a unicorn, you. The following four types of data can be distinguished, as made by Floridi (1999): (a) *primary data* is the main sort of data an information system is designed to convey; (b) *metadata*, when data is about data. For example, the creation date or the creation place of another piece of data; (c) *operational data*, related to the usage, performance or command of the

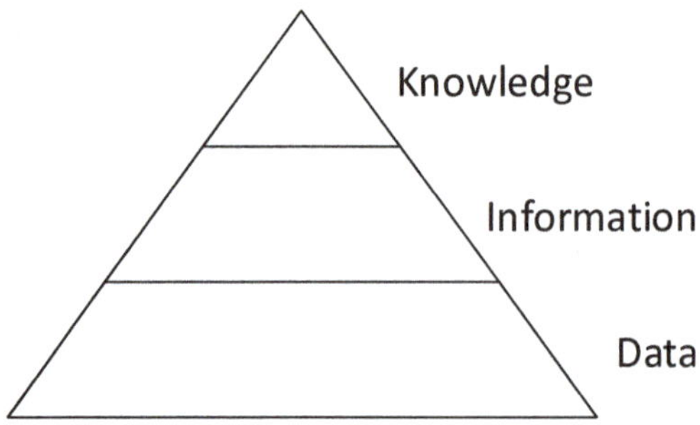

Fig. 1.1 Data, information and knowledge

information system and (d) *derivative data*, when data has been extracted from the other types of data. The consideration of what is data and what is metadata is inseparable from the use that is going to be made of it; and what is metadata for one receiver may well be data, and a valuable one, for another receiver. The same blurred frontiers exist among the other types of data.

Data are grouped in messages that transmit some *information* in a communication channel from a sender to a receiver. One single piece of data has value inasmuch as it can represent a message with meaning in a context, that is to say, convey information. In other words, data can be seen as information without meaning. Extracting information from data is not always an obvious task.

Through the study and interpretation of data it is sometimes possible to extract valuable information. When this information is considered during the course of a decision process, then that information is called *knowledge*, at least under the most utilitarian gnoseological dogma. If choice is an important element of democracy and decisions ultimately depend on data (processed either rationally or irrationally), we can conclude that data is at the base of democracy.

1.2.2 The Web as a Source of Data

In the World Wide Web, the pages that are visited when one does 'internet surfing' are a set of documents globally accessible and hosted in distantly located computers. These documents are text files in HTML format (richly formatted text), images, videos and small computer programs (scripts) among other file types. Documents are accessible because the variety of heterogeneous data transmission technologies, including optical fibre, radio links or network cables, observe the same standard protocols, thus enabling their interoperation.

The internet protocols determine that whenever somebody browsing a web (the client computer) types a web address in the web browser, like `http://site.com/page`, an internet address (IP address, from 'Internet Protocol' address) is returned from the name (`site.com`) and that computer (server) is contacted to retrieve the requested document. The protocol ruling the exchange of commands and documents between a client and a server in the web is the 'HTTP' (Hyper Text Transfer Protocol). The term *hypertext* makes reference to the fact that documents typically include links to other pages, either hosted locally in the same computer or remotely in another server.

The pieces of information in the Web are arranged as a complex network of interconnected *documents*, vaguely resembling the way neurons are connected in the human brain, or the way our ideas connect to other ideas. But the web is a source of extraordinarily valuable *data*. The documents in the web are rich in tables, diagrams, charts, infographics or simply numbers dropped among dull text paragraphs. These are all pieces of data. However, these data cannot be exploited in an efficient manner. First, because they are not always directly accessible. Some numbers may be given in a pie chart published as a raster image, and they can only be extracted with OCR (optical character recognition) techniques and with much uncertainty. Second, because sometimes data is published as text, but then it lacks context—it is not information but a collection of meaningless raw numbers. These pieces of raw data are useless for computer algorithms because they cannot be systematically extracted and processed.

Different pieces of data referring to the same entity are totally disconnected in the web of documents and they lack any link that permits increasing the knowledge on specific entities. Pieces of relevant data in distant locations cannot be thus automatically related or compared. Whenever global identifiers for entities do not exist or they are not used, matching pieces of information becomes a cumbersome task (e.g. Shakespeare, W. vs. *William Shakespeare*) and is prone to errors. In other occasions data is well structured in large raw files using well established identifiers (e.g. ISBN for books), but then they are offered as a bulk file for download, without the ability to be queried in individual accesses. A large file has to be downloaded before it can be processed, rendering unpractical its use.

The task of extracting data from Web resources can also be a hard one because data is offered in a myriad of formats, sometimes described in closed specifications and in any case specific for different domains and requiring dedicated processing.

All these hurdles make it difficult to effectively use the billions of pieces of data that as today—in one way or another—are present on the web. In practice, the potential of the web as a source of data is lost.

Publishers on the Web (from web bloggers to public institutions) are in general interested in publishing content as fast as possible whereas possible consumers of data on the Web would like to find carefully described and well formatted, high-quality data. There is an evident mismatch between occasional data producers and data consumers with no easy solution. Two opposite approaches have been proposed.

The first approach places the burden of work on the data consumer: content publishers are not going to make any effort without reward and data consumers have to assume they need intelligent tools and more clever search engines, capable of extracting information even from unstructured content. In a word, the first approach relies on Google being more intelligent every time. The second strategy consists of easing the task of high-quality publishing, providing a set of specifications and good practices for data to be on the web and trusting that at least a fraction of the data publishers will follow them.

None of these strategies has proved to be the ideal solution, but at least this second option offers the possibility of producing data within a larger web: the web of data. This chapter describes the new web of data relying on the specifications of the World Wide Web Consortium (W3C), and its most refined form, known as *linked data*.

1.3 Linked Data

Linked data is only the most refined form of publishing data on the web according to the W3C specs. The W3C describes 35 good practices for publishing data on the web (Farias et al. 2017), but only when networked in the web is its value fully realised. This data network is sometimes referred to as the 'Web of Data', a term with a more practical emphasis than the older but equivalent 'Semantic Web'. The '*Semantic Web*' was conceived in 1999 by Tim Berners-Lee, founder of the Web:

> I have a dream for the Web [in which computers] become capable of analysing all the data on the Web – the content, links, and transactions between people and computers. A 'Semantic Web', which should make this possible, has yet to emerge, but when it does, the day-to-day mechanisms of trade, bureaucracy and our daily lives will be handled by machines talking to machines. (Berners-Lee and Fischetti 1999)

Soon after, new technical specifications appeared striving to implement the Tim Berners-Lee dream. These specifications were not, however, aimed at creating an independent web but at improving the existing one:

> The Semantic Web is not a separate Web but an extension of the current one, in which information is given well-defined meaning, better enabling computers and people to work in cooperation. (Berners-Lee et al. 2001)

The new data network thereby created has started to grow slowly and silently. First, enthusiastic researchers and computer scientists started dumping datasets, then, public institutions followed; finally, for-profit companies joined the effort.

The Web of Data shares with the World Wide Web the same problems, deficiencies and challenges: the information quality is highly irregular, its availability too unstable and the credibility of the sources uncertain. But few questions that the Web of Data is the seed of a new paradigm where humans are giving way to machines in the use of the internet; and a new sphere of communications where both senders and receivers are intelligent machines and humans play a lesser role.

1.3.1 Universal Identifiers

The first key idea of the Semantic Web is that every entity—animate or inanimate, particular or abstract—is liable to have an identifier: the universal resource identifier universal resource identifier or URI. Data in the Web of Data refer to entities very precisely identified.

URI s are sequences of characters with several parts separated by dots and slashes. For example, URLs (universal resource locator), which are the web addresses that are introduced in a web browser to get a page, are also a kind of URIs. This coincidence that makes URIs to be a superset of the URLs is not accidental: an expected behaviour of typing a URI in a web browser is that information on the identified object is retrieved. The string of characters used to identify a thing, magically retrieves more information on that thing if the HTTP protocol is used to query the right computer. We say that a URI *resolves* when it has the form of URL and it can be navigated.

Perhaps we have not appraised well enough the importance of the URIs as identifiers and their ambitions, for URIs aim at naming every object in the world in a uniform manner. Some people claim '*there is nothing in a name*', and a rose by any other name would smell as sweet. However, designating objects is not a neutral act—in other times this was a sacred act—and it reveals a specific worldview. URIs tend to assume simple hierarchical relations between authorities. For example, a fictitious domain `mydept.myorganisation.uk` actually embodies the idea of a Department (`mydept`) organically depending on a certain organisation (`myorganisation`) in turn located in the UK. Relations are not homogeneous (part-of vs. located-in) but suggest a tree structure. This tree structure is sometimes used to classify the type of resources described, in strings like `type_of_resource/identifier`.

The feature of URIs being at the same time both identifiers and the means to retrieve information in an easy manner is an invitation for information to be retrieved and the whole concept fosters fluent information flows.

1.3.2 Linked Data and RDF

The second key idea of the Semantic Web is that information can be given about any URI identifier. For example, Thomson Reuters, a giant company whose business is information, has collected a database of organizations from all over the globe called *permid*. In this database, each organization is identified by a URI. Thus, a fictitious company, let us say ACME Inc., is identified with the following URI: `https://permid.org/1-4296162760`.

If this URI (which is also a URL) is introduced in a web browser, a nicely laid out webpage will be displayed to the user. Actually, the web page is not impressive because there is not much information in the *permid* database: the headquarters address, the country where it is incorporated and a few other values. Other similar databases, like *crunchbase* or *opencorporates*, offer some more information, like the relevant shareholders or the people in executive jobs. However, *permid*'s ambition is big, as the ultimate purpose is ACME Inc. to be uniquely identified by the permid URI—replacing one of the functions of a public Commercial Registry. In some manner, this ambition is being fulfilled, as the acceptance of Thomson Reuters' ids has not stopped growing.

But there is more. When a machine resolves that URI, specifically demanding data, the retrieved answer is not the beautifully formatted HTML document in the figure above. Rather, a succinct dataset is returned, in a much more precise and structured format. The next figure reproduces the text message that would obtain a machine in whose HTTP request headers the proper code is given.

```
@prefix tr-common: <http://permid.org/ontology/common/> .
@prefix fibo-be-le-cb:
<http://www.omg.org/spec/EDMC-FIBO/BE/LegalEntities/CorporateBodies/.
@prefix xsd:   <http://www.w3.org/2001/XMLSchema#> .
@prefix vcard: <http://www.w3.org/2006/vcard/ns#> .
@prefix tr-org: <http://permid.org/ontology/organization/> .

<https://permid.org/1-4296162760>
    a                            tr-org:Organization ;
    tr-common:hasPermId          "4296162760"^^xsd:string ;
    tr-org:hasActivityStatus     tr-org:statusActive ;
    tr-org:isIncorporatedIn      <http://sws.geonames.org/6252001/> ;
    fibo-be-le-cb:isDomiciledIn  <http://sws.geonames.org/6252001/> ;
    vcard:organization-name      "ACME Inc"^^xsd:string .
```

Details on the meaning of this piece of information are not relevant now, but the idea is that of having data describing an entity identified by an URI identifier. The URI `https://permid.org/1-4296162760` is special because it is being used deliberately to identify an entity and it is special because its resolution offers information suitable for both machines and humans.

The piece of data shown above is in a form known as linked data and it follows the best Web recommendations for publishing data online. It is not an Excel file, it is not an excerpt of a relational database. Instead, the piece of data above is RDF (*Resource Description Framework*). RDF is not a data format, but an information model which can be incarnated in different ways—for example XML or JSON. An RDF graph is a set of units of information known as RDF triples. Each of the RDF triples represents a sentence, an atomic unit of information linking three entities. These entities are known as subject, predicate and object, resembling the equivalent concepts in language studies.

In the daily use of language, however, we often use structures more complex than a subject, a verb and an object (like in *Heracles stole apples*). But we can always chain simple sentences to add information (and that *apples were golden*). Thus, using the constituents of one sentence in another sentence, arbitrarily complex pieces of information can be given. If we draw these relations, we see these RDF triples weave a web of connections. An example of RDF sentence, extracted from the ACME example, with a subject, a predicate and an object follows:

```
SUBJECT:    <https://permid.org/1-4296162760>
PREDICATE: <http://www.w3.org/1999/02/22-rdf-syntax-ns#type>
OBJECT:     <http://permid.org/ontology/organization/Organization>
```

The first line above is the subject, and it is a URI identifying ACME. The second line is the predicate meaning 'is a kind of'. Finally the third line, the object, is URI representing the abstract concept of "organization". We may understand this RDF triples means 'ACME is an organization'.

Let us imagine that the Thomson Reuters' *permid* database of organizations exactly devotes 6 RDF triples to ACME. These 6 triples are represented in the following code excerpt; each of the RDF triples has been shown separated by a blank line. The subject in all the triples is `<https://permid.org/1-4296162760>`, which is the URI of ACME in the permid database. The predicate is also a URI in each of those 6 cases, including words like type, `hasActivityStatus`, or `isIncorporatedIn`—words follow each other without blank space because they are not allowed in URIs. Finally, the object in each of the RDF triples is either a URI or a value, the former given between angle brackets and the latter given between quotation marks. Values are also known as constants or literal values.

```
<https://permid.org/1-4296162760>
<http://www.w3.org/1999/02/22-rdf-syntax-ns#type>
<http://permid.org/ontology/organization/Organization> .

<https://permid.org/1-4296162760>
<http://permid.org/ontology/organization/hasActivityStatus>
<http://permid.org/ontology/organization/statusActive> .

<https://permid.org/1-4296162760>
<http://www.omg.org/spec/EDMC-FIBO/BE/LegalEntities
       /CorporateBodies/isDomiciledIn>
<http://sws.geonames.org/6252001/> .

<https://permid.org/1-4296162760>
<http://permid.org/ontology/organization/isIncorporatedIn>
<http://sws.geonames.org/6252001/> .

<https://permid.org/1-4296162760>
<http://permid.org/ontology/common/hasPermId>
"4296162767"^^<http://www.w3.org/2001/XMLSchema#string> .

<https://permid.org/1-4296162760>
<http://www.w3.org/2006/vcard/ns#organization-name>
"ACME Inc"^^<http://www.w3.org/2001/XMLSchema#string> .
```

The six RDF triples above can be represented in an informal, visual manner in Fig. 1.2. Resources are represented as ovals, literals with rectangles. Every triple is represented as an arrow, where the subject of the triple is the origin and the object the destination. Prefixes have been used to shorten the URIs.[1]

There are some rules, a few, determining how a RDF triple can be built—the minimal information unit in the web of data. One of these rules determines that subjects and predicates in the RDF triples must be URIs, whereas objects can be either URIs or literal values. Nothing prevents a URI appearing in a triple as subject to be part of another RDF triple as object, or vice versa. In the sentence ‘Heracles stole the apples’, ‘the apples’ are the direct object (object in RDF terminology), but the same apples are the subject in the second exemplary sentence (the apples are gold). Given that URIs can represent any conceivable entity (resource) and given that RDF triples can be chained once and again, we can say that RDF can express any thing about anything. Humans are able to convey much more information with hardly a few words, but this is due to the fact that we humans share an implicit

[1] https://www.w3.org/TR/xml-names.

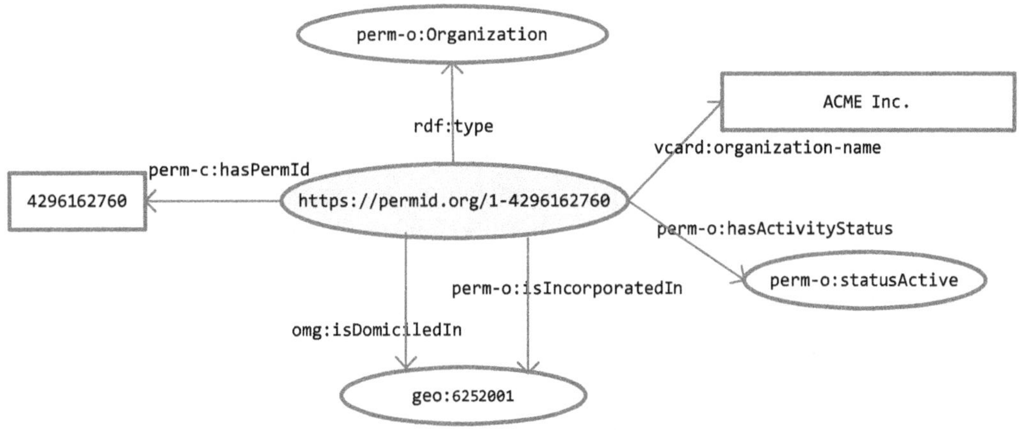

Fig. 1.2 Six RDF triples represented in a diagram

context, a background knowledge known to both emitter and receiver. But nothing, at least in theory, would prevent this context to be codified with another set of RDF triples.

Entities mentioned in an RDF graph can refer to both general ideas and specific individuals. The following code excerpt displays two out of the six RDF triples mentioned before, in the same format where each RDF triple is a set of three lines (S-P-O) separated from the next RDF triple by a blank line.

```
<https://permid.org/1-4296162760>
<http://www.w3.org/1999/02/22-rdf-syntax-ns#type>
<http://permid.org/ontology/organization/Organization> .

<https://permid.org/1-4296162760>
<http://www.w3.org/2006/vcard/ns#organization-name>
"ACME Inc"^^<http://www.w3.org/2001/XMLSchema#string> .
```

The meaning of the first triple is 'ACME is an organization'. The second triple means 'ACME has by organization name ACME Inc.'. ACME can be a real and concrete organization, whereas organization is just an abstract concept. In fact, 'organization' is a common noun while ACME is a proper noun.

Some philosophers in the past debated about the real existence of these abstract concepts—like organization—and posed the so called problem of the universals. Thus, the realist school claimed that universals were real, they existed and they were different from the particulars instantiating them. On the contrary, the nominalists denied the existence of universals both in an immanent manner (in the particulars) and in a transcendent manner (out of the particulars). In RDF, which is nothing but a language, both universals and particulars are in the same plane and there is no specific difference: a URI can identify both abstract concepts (organization, city) and concrete concept (Heracles, Japan) without any explicit reference to their nature.

1.3.3 Data Models, Ontologies and Ontology Design Patterns

The distinction between concrete things (the zip code of the ACME headquarters) and abstract concepts (the idea of organization) is syntactically non-existent in RDF. However, we shall distinguish between pieces of *data* and the *terms* of a vocabulary.

Any URI can be used in any RDF triple without further limitation. However, URIs with general ideas such as ‘organization’ are usually URIs which have been attributed more properties somewhere else, such as a definition, its relation with other similar concepts, its constituents or other properties inherent to its nature. Very often, the person or entity specifying the knowledge about a concept proceeds in the same manner with other concepts in the same domain, covering a specific area of interest and building one domain vocabulary. The complexity of vocabularies varies between a mere list of concepts and a complete ontology with a large amount of knowledge having been specified.

Gruber defined ontology as an ‘explicit specification of a conceptualization’ (Gruber 1993), Studer as ‘a formal, explicit specification of a shared conceptualization’ (Studer et al. 1998). Both definitions speak about conceptualizations made explicit, and the language to make them explicit today is OWL. An OWL (Web Ontology Language) ontology is asserted as a set of RDF triples, and it is, in fact, an ontology in the philosophical sense of the word, for it describes a collection of beings and their properties and relations. Ontologies can cover the whole universe of knowledge, or they can be limited to a specific area. In the latter case they are known as domain ontologies. Ontologies aiming at describing any piece of human knowledge can become huge: for example CYC keeps one of the largest knowledge base in the world and it describes several hundreds of thousands of terms carefully organized (Matuszek et al. 2006), competing with Yago (Suchanek et al. 2007) and others. On the contrary, domain ontologies can be as small as a few dozen triples. Some of these ontologies are mere catalogues of lexical resources. For example, WordNet (Miller 1995) comprises one hundred thousand terms, including nouns, verbs and adjectives. Nouns are related to other nouns that are hyperonyms, hyponyms, meronyms or holonyms.

Ontologies can cover different needs, from representing the consensus in a certain domain (namely, keep a list of definitions), to determining the execution of a computer application. In the latter case, the knowledge base is conceptually divided into two large blocks: the block with terminological information (or T-Box) and the block with information about the individuals instantiating those abstract concepts (A-Box).

There are multiple ways of modelling a reality with ontologies. Likewise, there are multiple ways of implementing an algorithm or designing a relational database. However, it is a good practice to solve recurrent problems with common solutions, because the solutions will have been tested, because others can better understand one’s work and because there is no need to reinvent the wheel. Much like using *design patterns* is a common practice among software engineers, *ontology design patterns* (ODP) should be a common practice among ontologists.

Ontology Design patterns were proposed in 2005 by Gangemi, and since their inception a few dozen have been described and published online, with the sole purpose of being reused as building blocks. Their influence, however, is unquantifiable, as the use of patterns is never acknowledged and probably less than what was expected. The reuse of individual terms have been fostered more actively by search engines (`http://vocab.cc`) and ontology repositories (`https://lov.linkeddata.es`). Indeed, ontologies have been defined in the legal domain.

1.3.4 Features of the Semantic Web

In linguistics, semantics is the science that studies the meaning of symbols. If we hear an ambulance siren wailing, we will probably interpret that a sick person is traveling inside. If we use now the ACME identifier (`https://permid.org/1-4296162760`), the careful reader will know that the headquarter is in the state of Michigan in the United States. The communication of a set of RDF triples from one agent (man or machine) to another agent is an act of communication and therefore words like 'syntax' or 'semantics' have full validity in this context.

The ACME URI is a linguistic sign, a signifier, which evokes a meaning (the idea of the company ACME). Computers with access to the web of data have a precise image of ACME, which can be accounted for, and it is indeed the information in the Thomson Reuters database and other possible mentions in the web of data. Computers might quantify how many facts they know about ACME. We, humans, are not able to determine what we know about ACME, nor the reactions that it provokes in us. Some will recall a bad experience with ACME, some will recall their favourite product from ACME; but no one will be able to know the subconscious.

The semiotic triangle of Ogden and Richards, applied to the human language, links three entities: the mental image (my idea of the ACME) with the sign (the sound of the word ACME Inc.) and both with the real object (the entity ACME). We may draw an equivalent semiotic triangle for the Semantic Web, as Sowa first suggested (Sowa 2010). Both are represented in Fig. 1.3, which adapts the figure in 'The Meaning of Meaning' by Ogden and Richards (1923).

The symbol invokes a meaning, the meaning refers to a referent. There is no direct relation between the symbol and the referent other than through the signified, which is an idea. Making it simpler and applied to the spoken language, the triangle puts in relation words with worlds with ideas—stressing the influence of language upon thought. In the human language, Saussure's concept of arbitrariness holds, and there is no direct connection between signifier and signified. Save for onomatopoeias, words do not resemble real objects. In the Semantic Web, the language

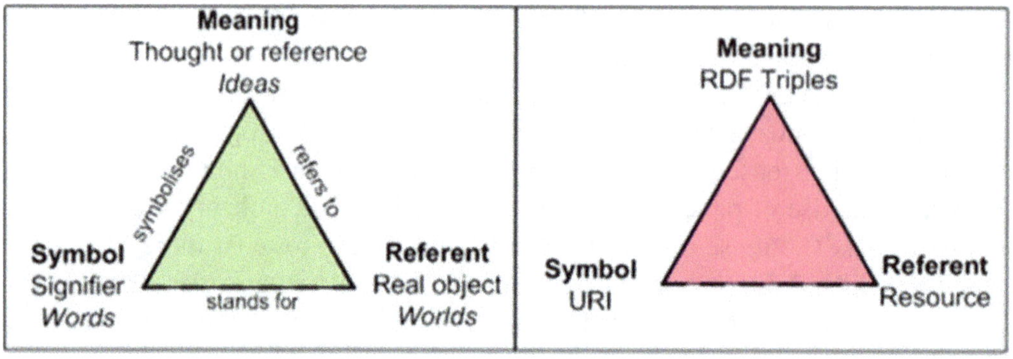

Fig. 1.3 Ogden and Richard's triangle adapted to the semantic web

is not entirely addressed to computers and symbols are not pure numbers but URIs with some words meaningful to humans in it.

Between humans, the relation between symbol and meaning is a complex one: the word "rain" may denote "drops of water falling" in its primary meaning, but it may connote "sadness and melancholy" in subjective meanings. As of today, machines can only denote primary meanings, and no computer has managed to emulate the richness of a human spoken communication, with all its ambiguities, double meanings and implicit connotations. Computers have not reached lyricism.

Syllogisms are structures of valid reasoning that were studied by Aristotle. Thus, if 'all men are mortal' and 'Socrates is a man', then we can derive that 'Socrates is mortal'. These two premises entail a conclusion. Each of the sentences represents some knowledge. We might say, that if we represented each of the two first sentences with a single RDF triple (and their simple structure favours that), we may deduce the third one. These kind of sentences are categorical propositions and their conveyed knowledge is limited to sentences of the sort 'some (or all) members of category A belong to category B'. But other kinds of reasoning are also possible.

In general, symbolic logic is the branch of science that studies valid forms of reasoning. Logic systems define a language, with an alphabet with symbols and some syntactic rules that determine which combinations of symbols are well formed. Logic systems also define inference rules, which can be applied to produce new formulas from existing ones. Valid reasoning only grants that false premises will never be derived from true premises—please note that truth and falsehood are attributes exclusive of the language, and the logical languages are simply languages. The concepts of truth and falsehood would not exist if there were no languages at all—the observation was made by Hobbes.

Computer ontologies have a logical foundation that enable some reasoning tasks. In particular, OWL ontologies are formalized as one of the Description Logics well described by Baader et al. (2003). The RDF triples can be the proposition in logical arguments that produce new RDF triples. One RDF triple may say that 'ACME is an organization'. One ontology may say that 'Organizations have Agents as members'. One reasoner may derive that Action has Agents as members. The millions of triples in the CYC ontology mentioned before might be used in complex reasoning. To date, there are not many computer applications using this powerful knowledge base, but the potential is huge.

The atomic units of information in the Semantic Web, namely, the RDF triples, do not live in a single location but they are distributed in computers all around the globe. With a uniform technology one can get access to either ontological assertions ('all men are mortal', 'organizations have agents as members') or to mere data ('Socrates is mortal', 'ACME has headquarters in Michigan') published by heterogeneous entities. Data is usually published as datasets, namely collections of registers about a topic in particular. Thus, the Thomson Reuters dataset on organizations has a dozen triples for each of the three million organizations they consider.

The peculiarity of the Semantic Web is that data are interconnected at a global level. The concept of publishing a collection of data is not a novelty, but the concept of publishing a collection of data massively connected to data and vocabulary terms published by others, certainly is. Let us consider as an example one of the RDF triples mentioned above:

```
<https://permid.org/1-4296162767>
<http://www.omg.org/spec/EDMC-FIBO/BE/LegalEntities/CorporateBodies/isDomiciledIn>
<http://sws.geonames.org/6252001/> .
```

This RDF triple can be interpreted as ACME is a legal entity domiciled in a certain place identified by geonames. The idea of 'domicile' is invoked using an identifier published by a third entity. This triple thus links three entities whose definitions are given by computers in London, Massachusetts (USA) and Bayern (Germany). Two of them belong to private companies (Thomson Reuters and Unxos), the third one to a not-for-profit technology standards consortium (OMG). In the other triples describing ACME, some more vocabulary terms and data are referred (defined for example by W3C).

The data published by geonames about the referred entity available under `http://sws.geonames.org/6252001/`, namely the USA, happens to be exactly 167 RDF triples, with information like the name of the place in different languages, or different coordinates with geolocation. Some of these 167 triples declare that the entity (USA) matches other records in other datasets, like DBpedia (Auer et al. 2007). DBpedia is a dataset published by an association (located in Leipzig) which publishes data extracted from Wikipedia as RDF. DBpedia is the only link that geonames makes to external data source, but the metadata refers to other external data, such as the Creative Commons license. The Creative Commons license is expressed with 90 RDF triples, and it is a dead end in the sense that no further datasets are linked from it. The information about the USA in DBpedia consists of 260 triples densely linked to other datasets published by different sources, like Eurostat, CYC or Freebase (Bollacker et al. 2008)—the number of accessible triples in a second level is already high.

DBpedia is actually massively linked by other datasets—even permid in some of their registers. Given that datasets (and vocabularies) reference each other, we may

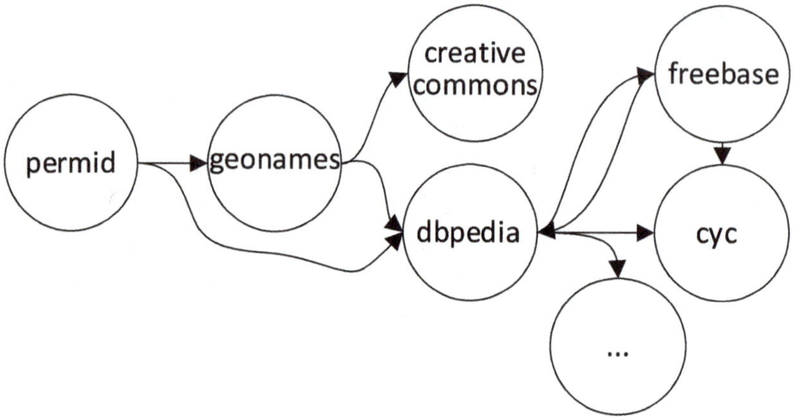

Fig. 1.4 Reference relations between several datasets

think of a graph, a data structure defined by nodes and edges that link them. These edges are directed, namely, they have a direction (for example from permid to geonames, but not vice versa). If we draw each dataset as a node and each connection between two datasets as an edge, we may create a figure as follows (Fig. 1.4).

If a dataset has their entities dereferenceable (the URIs identifying entities resolve with data when properly browsed with the HTTP protocol) and if these entities are linked to other datasets, then the dataset qualifies to be part of the Linked Open Data cloud (LOD). This data is better known then as linked data (the O in the LOD making reference to the idea of open standards, rather than data being openly licensed).

The datasets linked in the LOD cloud has not stopped growing in the last few years. The number of datasets is now so high that it cannot be comfortably fitted into a sheet of paper or a slide in a presentation—like the Tim Berners-Lee presentation shown in the next image. DBpedia is still represented at the center of these diagrams. Not in vain, many see in Wikipedia the Universal Encyclopedia that was at the core of H. G. Wells's book the World Brain (Wells 1938).

1.3.5 Rights in the Web of Data

RDF is mostly used to represent facts, positive assertions that can be either true or false, like the sentence 'Heracles stole apples'. But we humans also use other types of expressions, referring to what can be done, to what must be done and to what must not be done. These permissions, obligations and prohibitions are called deontic expressions and can be also represented in RDF with proper vocabularies.

For example, the well-known Creative Common licenses have been also represented as RDF by the Creative Commons foundation using their own vocabulary, which declares some terms such as `cc:Prohibition` or `cc:Permission`.

The Creative Commons vocabulary defines the necessary terms to represent the most important concepts in Creative Commons licenses, but it does not aim any further. Other vocabularies are more general, and rights can be in general represented as linked data (Rodríguez-Doncel et al. 2013). Thus, the Open Digital Rights Language (ODRL) is a more versatile policy language intended to be used in different domains: financial information, content in mobile devices, ebooks, news and others. ODRL was first specified in 2000 as an XML language, but more recently, the W3C has extended the language and has included a RDF serialization based on an ontology (Ianella et al. 2018) in its latest version.

The ODRL language permits representing permissions, possibly subject to certain restrictions ('you have access to this file but only in France'), prohibitions ('do not make derivative works') and duties ('you must inform the licensor'); with remedies if rules are not satisfied and a complete suite of policy types suitable for agreements, offers of assets (possibly at a certain price) or privacy policies.

ODRL does not provide any mechanism to digitally enforce the rights, mostly because this operation is not usually feasible beyond the mere access control. Yet, the value of ODRL should not be underestimated, as it enables the automated processing and administration of rights, making easier the search-by-license feature (when looking for images in a Google search, images can be filtered by rights information), the reasoning on rights expressions (it is possible to compute whether two licenses are compatible or not, as shown by Governatori et al. in 2013).

Moreover, the mere existence of policy languages with regulatory power and their acceptance by internet users, is transforming the mere nature of law. The *pragmatic turn* (Casanovas et al. 2017), which considers users' needs and contexts to facilitate the automated interactive and collective management of knowledge, is likely to become an element of growing importance in a future linked democracy as described in the forthcoming chapters.

1.3.6 Government of the Semantic Web

The Semantic Web does not have a different physical infrastructure to the Web. Linked datasets, ontologies, vocabularies and other resources are said to be in the Semantic Web as long as they are published following the best recommendations of the W3C. There is no centralized authority for the Semantic Web other than the W3C as the editor of purely technical specifications.

Participants in the Semantic Web are companies, public institutions and individuals alike, and this does not seem to be problematic. Let us consider one of the RDF triples mentioned before.

```
<https://permid.org/1-4296162767>
<http://permid.org/ontology/organization/isIncorporatedIn>
<http://sws.geonames.org/6252001/> .
```

As we have seen before, the ACME location is given with a reference to an entity managed by geonames. Geonames.org is a website created by the effort of a single engineer, Marc Wick, that is now maintained by the Swiss company Unxos GmbH. Indeed, Unxos might stop providing the service, but this would eventually be a relatively small problem for Thomson Reuters (publisher of this RDF triple), as they would change the reference in a short time (possibly to a location in DBpedia).

Above geonames, there is only the upper domain manager, the one in charge of . org names. The `.org` domains depend directly on ICANN (Internet Corporation for Assigned Names and Numbers), who also manage the top-level domains in the hierarchical namespace of the Domain Name System (DNS) of the Internet. As ICANN is the entity who ultimately manages IP addresses and names on the Internet, it is a key institution for the internet and consequently for the Semantic Web too.

Legally, ICANN is a non-profit organization, with a mandate to implement from the US Department of Commerce. After 18 years, as of October 2016, changes have happened in order to transfer some of its management duties to multisector agents of the global community. This model, known as MSG or MSI (from multi-stakeholder governance model or initiative) and described by Savage and McConnell (2015) tries to involve the different stakeholders in the internet government, much like technical specifications on the internet that are often written collectively: this is the case of IETF (Internet Engineering Task Force) or the W3C (World Wide Web consortium), where a large community of companies, researchers and public institutions coexist in a relatively peaceful and productive relation. The MSG is further described in Chap. 5.

This wide and coordinated participation in the edition of rules is quite a rare case. If we make an analogy with the road traffic regulations, we should imagine taxi drivers, truck transporters, local police and Royal Automobile Club members discussing together and deciding on the traffic regulations that will apply next year.

The role of individuals is not minor in the Semantic Web. Many well-known vocabularies and ontologies are the result of the work of researchers working alone or crowd sourced by individuals. Sometimes two vocabularies overlap in scope, covering the same domain. Over time some will survive and some will fall into disuse, being ultimately abandoned and their publication discontinued. It is a notable fact that authority (whether the vocabulary is published by the W3C or by a single individual) is important but not totally determining in this struggle. Technical quality and popularity of the resources are sometimes more important factors than the pure argument of authority. For example, despite the huge investment made by Cycorp, manager of the CYC knowledge base, CYC is secondary to DBpedia, created by a collective effort of internet users. This parallels the case of Wikipedia and the Encyclopædia Britannica, the former being the fourth website most visited in the world and the latter having fallen into a relative digital oblivion.

1.4 Government and the Web of Data

1.4.1 Open Government Data

Governments are relevant but not dominant stakeholders in the Web of Data and their role has been so far more about producing than about exploiting it. The term Open Government Data (OGD) is often defined as 'data produced or commissioned by government or government controlled entities'.

Open Government Data is published in government Open Data portals, which offer thousands of datasets in an organized manner. These portals either actively request data from the different government departments and agencies or passively wait for them to send the datasets. Some of the most relevant portals are the US data portal (`https://www.data.gov/`) and the UK data portal (`https://data.gov.uk/`). Stemming from Obama's US Open Government initiative in 2009, the US data portal collects almost 200,000 datasets with the purpose "to increase public access to high value, machine readable datasets generated by the Executive Branch of the Federal Government". The UK data portal, which maintains about 40,000 datasets, was created "to help people understand how government works and how policies are made" and embraces very warmly the linked data principles for putting data on the web.

At least three reasons have been identified for opening government data: transparency (for citizens to know that the government is doing), releasing social and commercial value (assuming again the idea that data is an asset) and participatory governance (engaging citizens in decision making). The use of OGD for the latter purpose has also been studied. For example Davies (2010) takes a theoretical and empirical look to assess who is using OGD and for what purposes, in order to determine the possible implications for different models of democratic change and public sector reform. Shadbolt and O'Hara (2013) also evaluated the UK OGD portal, but participatory governance played a minor role. It is generally agreed that Open Data Government must satisfy at least the eight principles written in December 2007 by thirty open government advocates (including Lawrence Lessig, Tim O'Reilly or Aaron Swartz): that data must be complete, from primary sources, timely, accessible, machine processable, non-discriminatory, non-proprietary and license-free.

1.4.2 Linked Open Government Data

Indeed, not every piece of OGD follows the linked data principles. But some relevant datasets in the Linked Open Data cloud have been produced directly by public institutions and many others have been re-formatted by third parties. And even these third parties have been very often partners in publicly funded research projects—governments have been supporting the development of the Semantic Web, especially in Europe.

Besides OGD, there are many other datasets relative to local or national governments which have also been published. Actually, the whole scope of OGD has been questioned as to whether OGD should stand for "(open government) data" or "open (government data)" (Yu and Robinson 2011). In the latest radiography of the Linked Data Cloud, in 2014, 183 datasets were classified as "government-related", amounting to 18% of the total (Schmachtenberg et al. 2014). Some of the datasets include the Brazilian politicians (de Souza et al. 2013), the debates in the Italian legislative cameras, data from the Greek police (Bratsas et al. 2011) or European Parliament debates (van Aggelen et al. 2017), to name a few.

We may define the term *linked open government data* as the intersection between government data (which is itself only a fraction of eGovernment), linked data and open data.

1.4.3 eGovernment and eDemocracy

The concept of eGovernment is about the better provision of services by public sector organisations by using digital technologies. In a wider sense, and according to the World Bank, "e-Government refers to the use by government agencies of information technologies [...] that have the ability to transform relations with citizens, businesses, and other arms of government". eGovernment can benefit from Semantic Web technologies in many ways. As an example, RDF vocabularies for the definition of public services offered by municipalities in Europe may help migrants to recognize the same service that is differently named in different regions.

As of 2018, about 49% of European citizens have used at least once an online service offered by a public institution,[2] and there is a public determination towards increasing this rate. The implementation of eGovernment is systematically evaluated by the public authorities in Europe. For example, the eGovernment Benchmark Study[3] monitors the development of eGovernment in Europe, evaluating indicators such as the number of services online, their degree of transparency, or the ability to make administrative processes fully available online. Important declarations have been signed (like the *Tallinn Ministerial Declaration on eGovernment*) as well as specific action plans (*EU eGovernment Action Plan 2016–2020*). Thus, on March 2017, the *European Interoperability Framework* (EIF) was adopted, focused on making digital public services more interoperable. Interoperability in that EIF was understood at four different levels: legal interoperability (which exists when

[2]Eurostat Information Society Indicators, April 2018, https://ec.europa.eu/digital-single-market/en/graph-european-society-indicators.

[3]http://ec.europa.eu/newsroom/dae/document.cfm?doc_id=48587.

legislation does not impose unjustified barriers to the reuse of data), organizational interoperability (which exists when formal agreements rule cross-organisational interactions), semantic inteoperability (which exists when there is a common understanding of exchanged data) and technical interoperability (which exists when information systems allow the free flow of bytes). Whereas this chapter has focused on semantic interoperability, the overall schema is reviewed with more detail in Chap. 5.

When information and communication technologies are specifically applied to empower deliberative democracy, the term eDemocracy is used instead. In eDemocracy, citizens go online to communicate opinions or complaints to the public administrations. The term eDemocracy is the preferred one when information technologies are used in one of the following cases: (i) as tools to strengthen deliberative democracy; (ii) as tools to communicate to the public institutions any kind of complaints, preferences or incidents or (iii) as a space to exercise political rights and participate in the political life. We will also suggest in Chap. 5 to place these different regulatory dimensions under the provisions of the rule of law (i.e. the meta-rule of law).[4]

The Semantic Web technologies have been postulated as a helpful tool to retrieve some meaning out of the online chatter about politics (Hilbert 2009), and it has been said to support the self-organization of people with joint political goals. For example, Belák and Svátek (2010) provided a core ontology for the description of political programs, commitments and trust between people. This work helps people to analyze, compare and discuss political programs, already in great databases like the Manifesto Project. The Manifesto Project offers the policy positions of parties derived from a content analysis of their electoral manifesto, covering over 1000 parties from 1945 until today in over 50 countries (Volkens et al. 2016). Similarly, the Constitute Project[5] (Elkins et al. 2014), offers as RDF, almost every constitution which has been in force anywhere in the world in the past 200 years. Legislation is offered as linked data in the UK and the Netherlands, with partial engagement also in the USA (Casellas et al. 2011a, b) and Canada (Desrochers 2012) and non-official support in many other countries.

However, there is also a reasonable concern about these tools and datasets remaining at a technical level, without actually reaching the masses. For example, the Linked Leaks datasets, containing information about 200,000 offshore entities that were part of the Panama Papers investigation, were released in 2016 as richly linked data; yet they have not been widely used.

---

[4]See Casanovas (2015), and Casanovas et al. (2016) for a comprehensive state of the art of Semantic Web applications in the legal domain.

[5]`http://www.constituteproject.org/`.

1.4.4 The Open Data Principles

Most of the data in the Linked Open Data cloud has been published as open data, namely, licensed under very liberal terms. This is the most natural option, as in the Web of Data building on others' resources is the most common practice.

The limits for what is considered open data and what is not open data have been well defined. Open data is data that anyone can access, use and share, according to the Open Data Institute (ODI) whereas openness is defined by Open Knowledge Foundation (OKFN) as situations when anyone can freely access, use, modify and share for any purpose (subject, at most, to requirements that preserve provenance and openness). Both OKFN and ODI have listed the well-known licenses (e.g. from Creative Commons or Open Data Commons) that comply with their definitions and have created visual labels to be easily recognized. In essence, open licenses grant that data can be used without legal barriers.

In the collective conscious, the open software movement has been associated with individual champions such as Linus Torvalds, Richard Stallman or Aaron Swartz. However, the open data movement is being promoted by global institutions. For example, the Group of Eight (G8) has signed in 2013 the "G8 Open Data Charter" outlining a set of five core open data principles to be followed by governments, the World Bank has devoted large resources to promote the adoption of the open data principles and the United Nations has drafted a development agenda called UN Data Revolution largely based on open data. Consistently, governments of most countries have enacted laws for publishing public sector information as open data, under the general principle that data produced with public funding must be openly published.

Open data has some downsides, though. First, it might favour inequality as the strongest become stronger. In theory, individual citizens have free access to information. In practice, only large companies with data science teams can extract actual value from it. These companies will leverage the open data resources for their own benefit, to the detriment of the rest. Second, the risk of re-identifying individuals in anonymised personal data is higher. The fact is that whereas the open data movement is energetically supported by public institutions, internet users and citizens in general have shown little enthusiasm.

1.4.5 Business Intelligence in the Public Sector

In the last decades, the relevance of data has increased as more and more decisions have been entrusted to computers and decision support systems.[6] Many large

[6]For a review of decision support systems using the Web of Data as presented in this book, see Blomqvist (2014).

companies make their biggest corporate decisions based on the results of complex computer processes that chew tons of apparently worthless data —this is known as *business intelligence* (BI).[7]

Decisions are usually taken as a result of a process in which different sorts of questions have to be answered. First, *descriptive* questions portray a certain reality (what is happening? how much? when? where?). In a second place, *diagnostic* questions look for explanations (why something has happened?). Then, *predictive* questions help forecasting the future (what will happen if I don't do anything?). Finally, *prescriptive* questions determine the best possible action (what should I do?). These answers can feed either a *decision support system*, where the ultimate decision is taken by a human, or a *decision automation system* where actions are executed without human intervention. Some data analytics applications stop at the descriptive stage, some power fully automated systems, like the management systems of the stocks of a retailer.

Most of the data that a company bases its decisions upon (like figures of sales or the customers' location) have an intrinsic value that is zealously protected—they are an intangible asset and its dissemination may favour other competitors. Data, as a commodity, can be also traded in a data market ("*i.e. the marketplace where digital data is exchanged as products or services derived from raw data*")[8] in exchange for money. Data markets are being fostered by governments.[9]

But for several reasons, data can also be publicly available under open licensing modalities. Many of the datasets relevant to BI processes had been always available, although not digitally—only as printed statistical yearbooks or in other non-digital forms. In the last few years, data has been massively dumped in the web and its full potential is yet to be realized.

Public administrations lag behind in the application of business intelligence to their decisions and there is not much literature in the area.[10] However, intelligent analyses are quietly being used by public administrations for the better provision of the services they offer (e.g. a municipality optimally planning the transport system). The growth of the amount of available data and the advances of the Artificial Intelligence (AI) algorithms will enable business intelligence to play a more important role in the decisions taken by public administrations in the years to come.

These techniques introduce a slight novelty in a long-standing question: the relation between experts in possession of scientific knowledge and politicians. In the most simplistic approach, the politician takes decisions and the expert provides

[7]The term predates computers. Business intelligence was defined as "*the ability to collect information and react to it accordingly*" in Cyclopaedia of Commercial and Business Anecdotes, R. Millar Devens (1865).

[8]European Data Market study, SMART 2013/0063, IDC 2016.

[9]As an example, see "Building a European Data Economy", COMM(2017), 9 (final).

[10]See the overview of possible applications by Wowczko (2016) or how business intelligence is being applied by the public institutions in the UK (National Archives 2016).

technical advice on how to execute them.[11] But the progress of technology not only rationalizes the means to implement the decisions, but also reduces the scope of politics: some of the questions, originally entrusted to the political sphere, can be optimized as well. The space of pure political decision-making is thus reduced by technological advances. The novelty in this question is that experts are also being replaced, in many of their functions, by intelligent machines. Further, the role of *professional experts* is even further diminished, as the expertise of a crowd of non-professionals is now available in the Internet era.

1.5 Conclusion

Data plus the right algorithms equals *information*, the right information used in a decision-making process is *knowledge*—at least according to the data/information/ knowledge pyramid model. The power of algorithms is not usually in the hands of individuals, but of large corporations with server farms and dedicated professionals. These algorithms, as almost any other modern technology, are no longer used to control the natural world, but to control other humans. In particular, political campaigns all over the world have allegedly been in recent years strongly influenced by intense data analytics processes powerful enough to tilt the scale.

Before this gloomy scenario, an unexpected actor can still play a role: a cloud of linked data enabling distributed knowledge and facilitating collective intelligence. The Web of Data, and more specifically, the linked data cloud, is a growing universe of connected information published about any matter in any language and accessible by anyone. The open data movement, initially sparked to increase the transparency of public administrations, has gained momentum and its economic and social value is now fully revealed. Public administrations, large and small enterprises, foundations, universities and individuals alike are contributing to creating a web of data, sharing the features of the web that we know is heterogeneous and diverse.

Much of the open source and free software movements have yielded first-class, high quality operating systems such as Linux, and the idea of open content has led to the release of millions of works now published under Creative Commons licenses, the open data movement combined with the semantic web technologies is creating a new data resource available to all. Maybe in the future, machine learning and data mining algorithms running over this pool of data will be also standard tools in the hands of individuals or self-organised collectives.

[11]This decisionist model of the the relation between politicians and experts has been compared with the technocratic model and Dewey's pragmatist one by Habermas (1974).

References

Auer S, Bizer C, Kobilarov G, Lehmann J, Cyganiak R, Ives Z (2007) DBpedia: a nucleus for a web of open data. In: The semantic web. Springer, Berlin, pp 722–735

Baader F, Calvanese D, McGuinness D, Patel-Schneider P, Nardi D (eds) (2003) The description logic handbook: theory, implementation and applications. Cambridge University Press, Cambridge

Belák V, Svátek V (2010) Supporting self-organization in politics by the Semantic Web technologies. IFIP ePart, pp 1–8

Berners-Lee T, Fischetti M (1999) Weaving the web: the original design and ultimate destiny of the World Wide Web by its inventor, 1st edn. Harper, San Francisco

Berners-Lee T, Hendler J, Lassila O (2001) The semantic web. Sci Am 284(5):34–43. https://doi.org/10.1038/scientificamerican0501-34

Blomqvist E (2014) The use of semantic web technologies for decision support—a survey. Semant Web 5(3):177–201

Bollacker K, Evans C, Paritosh P, Sturge T, Taylor J (2008) Freebase: a collaboratively created graph database for structuring human knowledge. In Proceedings of the 2008 ACM SIGMOD Int. Conf. on Management of data. ACM Press, Vancouver, Canada, pp 1247–1250. https://doi.org/10.1145/1376616.1376746

Bratsas C, Alexiou S, Kontokostas D, Parapontis I, Antoniou I, Metakides G (2011) Greek open data in the age of linked data: A demonstration of LOD internationalization. Proc ACM WebSci 11:1–4

Casanovas P (2015) Conceptualisation of rights and meta-rule of law for the web of data, Democracia Digital e Governo Eletrônico (Santa Caterina, Brazil), vol 12. 2015: 18–41; repr. J Gov Regul 4(4):118–129

Casanovas P, Palmirani M, Peroni S, van Engers T, Vitali F (2016) Semantic web for the legal domain: the next step. Semant Web 7(3):213–227. https://doi.org/10.3233/SW-160224

Casanovas P, Rodríguez-Doncel V, González-Conejero J (2017) The role of pragmatics in the web of data. Pragmatics Law. Springer, Cham, pp 293–330

Casellas N, Vallbé JJ, Bruce TR (2011) From legal information to open legal data: A case study in us federal legal information. In: POGK 2011: The AAAI Fall symposium on open government knowledge: AI opportunities and challenges

Casellas N, Vallbé J-J, Bruce TR (2011) From legal information to open legal data: a case study in U.S. Federal legal information. SSRN Electron J. https://doi.org/10.2139/ssrn.1959931

Davies T (2010) Open data, democracy and public sector reform. M.Sc. dissertation, Oxford University

de Souza JF, Siqueira SWM, de Ramos Araújo L, Melo RN (2013) Providing information from Brazilian politicians using linked data. In: Cases on open-linked data and semantic web applications. IGI Global, 39–57

Desrochers P (2012) Recordkeeping and linking government data in Canada. IEEE Intell Syst 27 (3):50–53

Elkins Z, Ginsburg T, Melton J, Shaffer R, Sequeda JF, Miranker DP (2014) Constitute: the world's constitutions to read, search, and compare. Web Semant Sci Serv Agents World Wide Web 27:10–18. https://doi.org/10.1016/j.websem.2014.07.006

Farias B, Burle C, Calegari N (2017) Data on the web best practices. W3C Recommendation, 31 Jan 2017

Floridi L (1999) Philosophy and computing: an introduction. Routledge, London

Gangemi A (2005) Ontology design patterns for semantic web content. In: International semantic web conference. Springer, Berlin, pp 262–276

Goodwin T (2015) The battle is for the customer interface. Crunch Network, 3 Mar

Governatori G, Rotolo A, Villata S, Gandon F (2013) One license to compose them all. In: International semantic web conference. Springer, Berlin, pp 151–166

Gruber T (1993) A translational approach to portable ontologies. Knowl Acquisition 5(2):199–229

Habermas J, Lennox L, Lennox F (1974) The Public sphere: An Encyclopedia Article (1964). *New German Critique* (3):49. http://doi.org/10.2307/487737

Hilbert M (2009) The maturing concept of e-democracy: from e-voting and online consultations to democratic value out of jumbled online chatter. J Inform Technol Politics 6(2):87–110. https://doi.org/10.1080/19331680802715242

Ianella R, Steidl M, Myles S, Rodríguez-Doncel V (2018) ODRL vocabulary and expression 2.2. W3C Recommendation, 15 Feb 2018

Matuszek C, Cabral J, Witbrock MJ, DeOliveira J (2006) An introduction to the syntax and content of cyc. In: AAAI Spring symposium: formalizing and compiling background knowledge and its applications to knowledge representation and question answering, pp 44–49

McLuhan M (1964) Understanding media: the extensions of man. The New American Library, New York

Miller GA (1995) WordNet: a lexical database for English. Commun ACM 38(11):39–41

National Archives (2016) The digital landscape in government 2014–15 Bus Intell Rev. As of Apr 2017. Available at: http://www.nationalarchives.gov.uk/

Ogden CK, Richards A (1923) The meaning of meaning. Harcourt, New York

Rodríguez-Doncel V, Gómez-Pérez A, Mihindukulasooriya N (2013) Rights declaration in linked data. In: Hartig O et al (eds) Proceedings of the 3rd international workshop on consuming linked data (CEUR 1034)

Savage JE, McConnell BW (2015) Exploring multi-stakeholder internet governance. Brown University Bruce W. McConnell, EastWest Institute

Schmachtenberg M, Bizer C, Paulheim H (2014) Adoption of the linked data best practices in different topical domains. In: International semantic web conference. Springer, Cham, pp 245–260

Shadbolt N, O'Hara K (2013) Linked data in government. IEEE Internet Comput 17(4):72–77. https://doi.org/10.1109/MIC.2013.72

Sowa JF (2010) The role of logic and ontology in language and reasoning. Theory and applications of ontology: Philosophical perspectives. Springer, Dordrecht, pp 231–263

Studer R, Benjamins VR, Fensel D (1998) Knowledge engineering: principles and methods. Data Knowl Eng 25(1):161–198

Suchanek FM, Kasneci G, Weikum G (2007) Yago: a core of semantic knowledge. In: Proceedings of the 16th international conference on world wide web. ACM, pp 697–706. https://doi.org/10.1145/1242572.1242667

Van Aggelen A, Hollink L, Kemman M, Kleppe M, Beunders H (2017) The debates of the European Parliament as linked open data. Semant Web 8(2):271–281

Volkens A, Lehmann P, Matthieß T, Merz N, Regel S (2016) The Manifesto data collection. Manifesto Project (MRG/CMP/MARPOR)

Wells HG, Mayne AJ (1938) World brain. Methuen & Company

Wowczko I (2016) Business intelligence in government driven environment. Int J Infonomics 9(1). https://doi.org/10.20533/iji.1742.4712.2016.0134

Yu H, Robinson DG (2011) The new ambiguity of 'Open Government'. UCLA L Rev Discourse 59:178. https://doi.org/10.2139/ssrn.2012489

Chapter 2
Deliberative and Epistemic Approaches to Democracy

Abstract Deliberative and epistemic approaches to democracy are two important dimensions of contemporary democratic theory. This chapter studies these dimensions in the emerging ecosystem of civic and political participation tools, and appraises their collective value in a new distinct concept: linked democracy. Linked democracy is the distributed, technology-supported collective decision-making process, where data, information and knowledge are connected and shared by citizens online. Innovation and learning are two key elements of Athenian democracies which can be facilitated by the new digital technologies, and a cross-disciplinary research involving computational scientists and democratic theorists can lead to new theoretical insights of democracy.

Keywords Deliberative democracy · Epistemic democracy · Semantic web · Institutions · Participatory ecosystems

2.1 Introduction

Semantic Web engineers have often complained that building ontologies is hard. To build an ontology for a given domain—for example, tort law—one needs to recruit experts in that domain, elicit their legal knowledge, and then reach a shared, explicit consensus of how such legal knowledge will be represented and formalised so that computers can 'understand it'. It is not an easy task, indeed, especially if ontologies have to be designed from scratch and the subject matter is complex.

If it is hard to build ontologies, mapping the conceptual domain of deliberative and epistemic theories of democracy is not less harder. In fact, it is quite the opposite. In the last thirty years, political philosophers and scientists have produced an oceanic body of literature on the justification, mechanisms, and outcomes of democracy based on a number of procedural and cognitive arguments. They have done so at different levels: normative (discussing the foundational values), theoretical (formulating hypothesis), and empirical (developing case studies and testing new institutional arrangements). Successive generations of scholars have expanded,

M. Poblet et al., *Linked Democracy*, SpringerBriefs in Law,
https://doi.org/10.1007/978-3-030-13363-4_2

refined, or remixed their different approaches with extraordinary sophistication. As a result, any attempt to represent the domain of contemporary models of democracy will necessarily be limited and selective. Like the making of the 19th century Oxford English Dictionary, or the 21st century Wikipedia, the effort would require the involvement of hundreds if not thousands of dedicated volunteers.

This chapter will take an oblique route by briefly considering the debates in democracy theory over the last decades that have explored the meaning and practice of democratic participation. The discussions about the role of citizen participation are sometimes structured into a binary between 'procedural' and 'epistemic' accounts of democratic practice, or, with a different terminology, between 'majoritarian' and 'populist' approaches. Hélène Landemore has proposed a more expressive dichotomy: the 'talkers' and the 'counters' (Landemore 2013, 53).[1] The 'talkers' walk the path of 'deliberation followed by majority rule as a fallible but overall reliable way to make collective decisions'; the 'counters' explore 'the epistemic properties of judgement aggregation when large groups of people are involved' (Landemore 2013, 54–55). Yet, an analysis of the most recent literature will reveal that subsequent debates have reconciled aspects of these two positions as the impact of empirical research, developments in cognitive sciences and digital technologies have opened up new research questions.

In this chapter we will focus on the alignment between deliberative and epistemic democratic theory and practice in order to consider, in Chap. 3, the varieties of wider citizen participation promoted by digital platforms which, interestingly enough, are typically agnostic about these philosophical debates. The findings of both deliberative and epistemic theories will help us to develop a matrix of civic and political participation tools and will guide further research into technology-enabled democratic participation. From this standpoint, we will consider how our notion of 'linked democracy'—as a distributed, technology-supported collective decision-making process—can provide a framework to structure the current plurality of civil and political participation practices. Linked democracy is about turning this plurality into a participatory ecosystem where data, information, and knowledge are connected and shared. Drawing from the experience of both 'talkers' and 'counters', we will suggest that 'connectors' are also needed to make the most of distributed crowd intelligence. As Josiah Ober has shown with his insightful analysis of classical Athens, 'making good use of dispersed knowledge is the original source of democracy's strength' (Ober 2008a, 2). Our 21st century democracies have challenges that were absent in classical Athens, and scale is notably one of them. Yet, our democracies have tools to address them that are truly unique 21st century innovations. And both the similarities and the differences are fascinating to explore.

---

[1]As Landemore's book acknowledges Jacob Levy for suggesting this very decipherable dichotomy to her, we want to preserve the attribution chain and thank him as well.

2.2 Deliberative Approaches to Democracy

In the early 1990s, political theorists began to suggest an expanded role for citizens in democratic processes based on the principles of public deliberation (Benhabib 1996; Bohman 1996; Dryzek 1994; Estlund 1993, 1997). The so-called 'deliberative turn' went beyond an acceptance of democratic practice as the simple aggregation of voter preferences for representatives at elections. It was argued that 'deliberation' through public and individual reflection and dialogue should inform and transform voter preferences or judgments and thus collective decision-making. Deliberation is about 'processes of judgment and preference formation and transformation within informed, respectful, and competent dialogue' (Dryzek and Niemeyer 2010, 2). The ideal is that 'inclusive, non-coercive and reciprocal discussion' on relevant issues should influence 'individual preferences and shape public policy' (Kuyper 2015). Public deliberation by 'free and equal' citizens provides legitimation for political decision-making, therefore, justifications for proposed decisions, policies and laws need to be publicly given and debated to inform the voting public. This does not render voting (or the aggregation of preferences) as meaningless but situates it as 'a phase of deliberation' in a democratic process (Bohman 2009, 28).

The concept of deliberation is already present in Aristotle's writings and, according to Christian Koch, both deliberation (boulē, bouleusis) and deliberate choice (proairesis) are the key notions that 'link Aristotelian rhetoric, ethics, and politics together' (Koch 2014, 13).[2] Generally, Jensen Sass and John Dryzek (2014) acknowledge that 'deliberation' as a political concept extends from Athens to contemporary Western liberal democracies. While the modern literature on deliberative democracy offers many definitions of the term, Hélène Landemore notes that "the reasoning aspect of exchange of arguments" in Aristotle's deliberation resonates in the definition by Joshua Cohen (one of the early proponents of deliberative democracy), the 'public use of arguments and reasoning' (Cohen 1989, cited in Landemore 2013, 91).

Since the first formulations of the 'deliberative turn' in democracy theory, there have been a number of overlapping turns within the turn. As John Dryzek and Simon Niemeyer have synthesised, an 'institutional turn' has focused on small-scale deliberative forums; a 'systemic turn' has instead reflected on large-scale systems; a 'practical turn' has bridged the gap between deliberative democracy and real politics and, finally, an 'empirical turn' aims at refining the theoretical claims with empirical

[2] "Deliberation is the kind of reasoning that precedes deliberate choice, for which Aristotle's term is proairesis (…). Proairesis literally means 'taking something rather than (something else)'. What makes these concepts so important to Aristotle's ethical thinking is that the individual's deliberate choices are what primarily determines that individual's ethical worth. Rhetoric, however, is also about deliberate choice, but of a different kind, i.e., collective choices by people organized in groups like the polis. (Koch 2014: 13).

testing (Dryzek and Niemeyer 2010, 6–10). More recently, Stephen Elstub (2015) and Jonathan Kuyper (2015) have identified three similar turns or generations of deliberative democracy theories. Elstub distinguishes between (i) normative foundations as set by Habermas (e.g. 1985, 1991) and Rawls (1999, 2001); (ii) institutionalisation of deliberative democracy with inclusion of other types of communication beyond public reason (e.g. Bohman 1996; Gutmann and Thompson 1996; Sanders 1997; Young 2000), and (iii) empirical turn and institutional design (e.g. Dryzek 1994, 2002, 2006, 2010, 2013). Elstub also anticipates a fourth generation inspired by the leading work of Jane Mansbridge and John Parkinson on large-scale deliberative systems (Mansbridge and Parkinson 2012) and argues that, by becoming more pluralistic and fragmented, deliberative democracy has become much less distinctive as a theory but, at the same time, is adaptive to change in ideas and interpretations (Elstub 2015, 101). Similarly, Jonathan Kuyper considers the works of Jürgen Habermas and Joshua Cohen that explore the ideals of deliberative democratic practice as the first stage; in the second stage, research focuses on 'empirical and practical applications' to mediate theoretical positions with the realities of liberal democracies and to test claims for deliberative practices; in the current third stage, there is an attempt to accommodate the values as well as the means and ends of deliberative democracy into large-scale systems to develop a 'system-wide' model. Following the framework set by Mansbridge et al. (2012), Kuyper also suggests a system-wide model with many discrete but interconnected components cohering into a complex whole and proposes a 'division of epistemic labor' (Kuyper 2015, 55). Based on the assumptions that—no individual citizen is knowledgeable about all relevant issues, and has diverse interests and priorities as well as discrete areas of expertise—the model proposes that citizens can self-select or exit from a wide-range of discussions, polls, panels and problem-solving arenas. A high level of knowledge and competence amongst citizens is not a prerequisite for participation as epistemic diversity serves to address individual bias and enhance individual knowledge levels. In addition, non-deliberative events have an 'augmenting' or disruptive role and can contribute indirectly to a citizen's learning and decision-making ability. The primacy of 'rational deliberation' is downplayed in favour of 'layered deliberation' that accommodates a range of styles and levels as well as multi-site deliberation (Kuyper 2015, 60). Likewise, in a revision of previous models positing more restrictive definitions of deliberation (e.g. Dryzek and Niemeyer (2010) requiring authentic, inclusive and consequential components) Sass and Dryzek (2014) also seek to extend the notion of deliberation onto a cross-cultural landscape and identify examples in non-western contexts of practices that they consider 'deliberative', but not necessarily consequential. This extended coverage also reveals how influential the deliberative paradigm and its multiple forks remain after more than two decades, inspiring institutional innovations that are currently deployed across the world.

2.2.1 Deliberative Democracy in Action: Some Institutional Innovations

The empirical turn in deliberative democracy has sparked a number of institutional innovations that are currently being deployed and replicated at different levels of governance in many democratic countries. These innovations, usually referred to as 'mini-publics' (Goodin and Dryzek 2006; Geissel and Newton 2012; Gröndlund et al. 2014), involve randomly-selected microcosms of citizens that are convened to deliberate on public issues.[3] As Robert Goodin and John Dryzek put it, mini-publics are 'designed to be groups small enough to be genuinely deliberative, and representative enough to be genuinely democratic (though rarely will they meet standards of statistical representativeness, and they are never representative in the electoral sense)' (Goodin and Dryzek 2006, 220).

The expression 'mini-publics' is an umbrella term that covers a variety of deliberative entities, some of them already in place before the 'deliberative turn'. As Gröndlund et al. note (2014, 2), Citizen Juries (in the US), Consensus Conferences (in Denmark) or Planing Cells (in Germany) have existed since the 1970s, while Deliberative Polls © (DP) and 21st Century Town Meetings © are newer designs. In their review of definitions of mini-publics, Matthew Ryan and Graham Smith distinguish between (i) restrictive definitions focusing exclusively on Deliberative Polls (Fishkin 2009); (ii) intermediate definitions including citizens' assemblies, citizen juries, planning cells, consensus conferences, and 21st Century Town Meetings (Goodin and Dryzek 2006); and (iii) expanded definitions that cover participatory budgeting and community meetings (Fung 2003; Ryan and Smith 2014, 12). In a previous account, Graham Smith also distills the common design features of 'mini-publics': (i) use of random or quasi-random sampling techniques (sortition); (ii) short-time events (typically 2–5 days, with the exception of longer citizens' assemblies); (iii) facilitation of the debates by moderators in order to ensure procedural fairness; (iv) cross-examination of expert witnesses presenting evidence to citizens; (v) deliberation in plenary and/or small-group sessions (Smith 2012, 90). Likewise, most of them (although not DPs) may conclude with a report that summarises a number of recommendations to the convenors (Smith 2012, 91).

Let us briefly examine Deliberative Polls, which in the words of Mansbridge are 'the gold standard of attempts to sample what a considered public opinion might be on issues of political importance' (Mansbridge 2010, 53). The idea of DPs was initially conceived by James Fishkin in 1987 during his stay at the Stanford Center for Advanced Study in the Behavioral Sciences and went live one year later in the form of a 'National Issues Convention' broadcasted on a PBS television program

[3]In *After the Revolution*, political scientist Robert Dahl proposed to 'seriously consider restoring that ancient democratic device [lot] and use it for selecting advisory councils to every elected official of the giant polyarchy' (1970, 122–123) and, later on, he suggested the idea of deliberative 'mini-populi' in *Democracy and Its Critics* (Dahl 1989, 342).

(Fishkin 2009, x–xi). The process followed in DPs is best explained by Fishkin himself as he describes the election of the PASOK's (Greek Socialist Party) official candidate for mayor of Marousi (metropolitan Athens) in June 2006:

> First a random sample of a population (in this case eligible voters) responded to a telephone survey, then they were convened together for many hours of deliberation, both in small groups and plenary sessions, directing questions developed in small groups to competing candidates, experts, or policymakers in the plenaries, and then, at the end of the process, they filled out the same questionnaire as the one they had been given when they were first contacted in their homes. In this case, the questionnaires were supplemented with a secret ballot in a separate polling booth because the process was more than a poll. It was an official decision. (Fishkin 2009, 10)

To Mansbridge, DPs are 'are strongest in representativeness, very strong on outcome measurement, and equal to any other in balanced materials, policy links, and the quality of space for reflection' (Mansbridge 2010, 53). However, as governments, large foundations, or the media industry are the usual funding sources for DPs they also tend to 'not provide the deliberators with radical left or right alternatives that are not within the currently feasible political process' (idem). Relying on a previous typology of mini-publics (Elstub 2014), Marit Böker and Stephen Elstub argue that 'of the different types of mini-publics, DPs allow the least citizen control and decision making impact. Indeed, rather than opening up a space in which citizens can voice critique, the rationale for DPs typically focuses on changing, almost correcting, participants' views' (Böker and Elstub 2015, 134). The authors also review DPs and other mini-publics in the light of the selection method, activities, outputs and recipients of the outputs, and conclude that 'of the most common types of mini-publics, CCs [Consensus Conferences] and CAs [Citizen Assemblies] tend to have the greatest emancipatory potential based on these features, whereas DPs so far seem to have had the least' (Böker and Elstub 2015, 136).

Generally, DPs and other mini-publics have also been critically scrutinised from the point of view of legitimacy (even if they aim at greater representativeness, mini-publics have no delegate power and can't speak on behalf of the broader population), legitimation of intended policies, and misuse (of the process or the outcomes by the authorities that set the consultation process).

Without precluding the value of mini-publics for research or a variety of public purposes (such as influencing public debate), Cristina Lafont has recently challenged Fishkin's approach to DPs as a shortcut, proxy, or second best for realising the ideal of quality deliberation, yet at the expense of mass participation. Fishkin's approach is designed to tackle what he refers to as the 'trilemma of democratic reform': is it possible to design constitutional reform processes that are able to satisfy simultaneously the three key democratic principles of political equality, mass participation, and deliberation? To date, Fishkin acknowledges, any system attempting to fulfill any of two principles inevitably misses the third: political equality and mass participation deny deliberation (there are no incentives to consider competing arguments); deliberation and mass participation deny political equality (participants may be self-selecting and not representative); political equality and deliberation deny mass participation (numerically impossible). The 'trilemma' is that all three principles cannot be achieved simultaneously (Fishkin 2011, 248). For Fishkin, deliberative microcosms (and DPs in particular) operate as a remedial modality to address these tensions, the rationale being—if a microcosm were chosen on the same principles of random survey participants, it offers a scaled version of a deliberative polity that is generalizable to the wider population. It is this scaled version that raises Lafont's concerns. First, following a previous point made by Parkinson (2006), she argues that members of deliberative microcosms 'participate as individual citizens with total freedom to express whichever views and opinions they have and to change them in whichever way they see fit. But, for that very same reason, they are in no way accountable to citizens outside the poll group' (Lafont 2015, 52). Second, Lafont suggests that 'deliberative democrats should welcome the proliferation of empirical research on micro-deliberative innovations, so long as it is not accompanied by the proliferation of the normative view that mass participation in quality deliberation is optional or dispensable for the realization of deliberative democracy' (Lafont 2015, 59).

However, and from a sociological perspective, Caroline Lee makes the opposite claim. In her book *Do-it-yourself democracy*, an account of a five-year fieldwork research on participatory processes in the US, she points out the pitfalls of what she refers to as 'the expanding market for public participation' and the role of engagement experts and facilitators (Lee 2015, 4). While recognising the positive effects of public participation events, she also argues that these may be only short-term, leading to the paradox of 'how public engagement can be authentically real and disempowering at the same time' (Lee 2015, 29) as the demands on citizens' time and commitment are not matched with actual impact on decision making and public policy.

Despite the generally admitted shortcomings of mini-publics when it comes to meet the normative, aspirational standards of deliberative democracy, there is a widespread agreement about their empirical value or the role they play in refining the theoretical underpinnings of the deliberative paradigm. For example, for Böker and Elstub 'mini-publics have been the democratic innovation from which the majority of empirical evidence on deliberative democracy has derived' (Böker and Elstub 2015, 130). Embracing the recent 'systemic turn', Böker and Elstub conclude that 'the systemic perspective that promises to subject future experimentation with mini-publics to a dynamic democratic momentum marks nothing less than the cutting edge of recent deliberative democratic theory' (Böker and Elstub 2015, 140). The steps that Böker and Elstub propose are:

> First, mini-publics can be evaluated and re-designed towards greater citizen control over the process, more open types of outputs, and more direct channels to formal decision-making. Second, the practice of mini-publics ought itself to be subjected to bottom-up deliberative processes. By conceptualising mini-publics as part of an overarching network of deliberative exchanges that evaluate and respond to one another, the emphasis shifts towards the establishment of a generally more active, transparent, and democratic system, whose ongoing evolution need not depend on top-down steering and control. (Böker and Elstub 2015, 140)

In a similar vein, Kuyper has also proposed a system-wide model with many discrete but interconnected components cohering into a complex whole and proposes a 'division of epistemic labor' (Kuyper 2015, 55). To be sure, the system-wide model of deliberation provides a conceptual conduit towards the research that has considered the nature and impact of 'collective intelligence' and 'distributed knowledge' and the role of networked public spaces in political decision-making. In the next section we review the arguments mobilised by contemporary theorists of epistemic democracy that have re-interpreted 'epistemic' in light of a new research emphasis on distributed knowledge and collective intelligence.

2.3 Epistemic Approaches to Democracy

The contemporary origins of epistemic approaches to democracy are interweaved with those of deliberative democracy and, in fact, they have evolved in the same way. The dichotomy between 'talkers' and 'counters' might eventually be more apparent than real as the two paradigms diversify and overlap. This may create some confusion to readers. For example, Joshua Cohen is often quoted as one of the leading proponents of deliberative democracy but his seminal 1986 paper is titled 'An epistemic conception of democracy'. In this paper, Cohen presents 'an epistemic interpretation of voting' with three components: '(1) an *independent standard* of correct decisions—that is, an account of justice or of the common good that is *independent* of current consensus and the outcome of votes; (2) a *cognitive* account of voting—that is, the view that voting expresses beliefs about what the correct policies are according to the independent standard, not personal preferences for policies; and (3) an account of *decision making* as a process of the adjustment of beliefs, adjustments that are undertaken in part in light of the evidence about the correct answer that is provided by the beliefs of others.' (Cohen 1986, 34). Cohen, however, would eventually abandon this explicit formulation, and hence the potential confusion. Melissa Schwartzberg has helped to clarify this issue by noting that 'as Cohen wrote the essay he had become skeptical about the idea that democracy was fundamentally about aggregating opinions about the content of the 'independent standard' (Schwartzberg 2015, 189).

Another issue about the 'independent standard of correctness' is that there are different versions of this core theoretical tenet in the epistemic democracy literature. As David Estlund explains, 'one version might say that there are right answers and that democracy is the best way to get at them. Another version might say that there are right answers and there is value in trying collectively to get at them whether or not that is the most reliable way. Yet another: there are no right answers independent of the political process, but overall it is best conceived as a collective way of coming to know (and institute) what to do. There are others' (Estlund 2008, 1). The more pragmatic approaches to the standard seem to have prevailed, though. Jack Knight has recently conceded that 'there's a growing number of people who probably think that getting at 'the truth' is too strong a claim to make for democratic institutions, but who do think that democracy has epistemic value in producing better decisions. Here the 'better decisions' would mean the enhancement of democratic decisions through discussion' (Knight et al. 2016, 138). Knight's last sentence also offers an additional clue by highlighting the role of deliberation in the contemporary epistemic approaches. In her account, Schwartzberg states that epistemic democracy emerged as a response to social choice theory to defend 'the capacity of 'the many' to make correct decisions' (Schwartzberg 2015, 187–188) and remarks that 'epistemic democracy does not position itself as an alternative to deliberative democracy but instead generally resituates deliberation as instrumental to the aim of good, or correct, decision making' (Schwartzberg 2015, 189).[4] Similarly, Landemore argues that 'epistemic democracy is both a subset of deliberative democracy and goes beyond it because it includes things that deliberative democracy doesn't necessarily include' (Knight et al. 2016, 142). According to Landemore, the epistemic models aim "to emphasize the knowledge-producing properties of democratic institutions and procedures; and specifically (…) to assume that those procedures are good at tracking a procedure-independent standard of correctness, which is sometimes called 'truth'" (Knight et al. 2016, 141).

Most contemporary epistemic democrats, in short, assume an independent standard of correctness in their models, but they do so in different ways. Depending on how it is formulated, democratic decision making will produce 'true', 'right', 'good', 'correct' or 'better' outcomes (provided that appropriate mechanisms are in place, as we will see). Regardless of the tonality that the standard adopts, it is hardly surprising if this is the cause of major theoretical debates. Can we rely on independent standards of what is true, or right, or good, or better, when diversity of opinions, values, and interests are the fabric of our plural democracies? If that is the case for some questions (let us say, questions involving core democratic principles or values) but not for others, how do we discern between them? As Schwartzberg put is, 'there may not be such an independent standard of correct decisions—or if such standard exists, we might not have any way of knowing whether we had reached it.' (Schwartzberg 2015, 198). Or, alternatively, in Landemore's view, it is possible for epistemic-democratic theories to 'conceptualize the truth, goodness, or correctness of democratic decisions or solutions' through diverse options: 'you can conceptualize it in terms of good governance, human rights, social justice, perhaps a developmental index, a happiness index or something like that, or something else entirely.' (Knight et al. 2016, 143). From this perspective, political scientists and social sciences in general could contribute to measure those achievements even though, as Nadia Urbinati objects, 'the measurement is always open to judgment and my judgment can be different from yours because in the domain of political

[4]In a similar vein, Estlund acknowledged that group dynamics could produce 'pathologies' leading to catastrophic decisions and insisted that this could mediated by 'proper deliberative procedures' and decision evaluation (Estlund 2008: 2). Ron Levy also suggests that the binary tensions that result from counterposing different governance models are 'to some extent illusory' as some accommodations can develop models which simultaneously encourage procedures, participation and deliberation (Levy 2013, 355).

opinion we don't have a mathematical measurement after all' (Knight et al. 2016, 149). The lack of conclusive answers or still insufficient empirical support leads Schwartzberg to conclude that epistemic democrats 'may wish to temper the strength of their claims' and that 'relinquishing the independent standard of correctness ought to be a first step' (Schwartzberg 2015, 201).[5] Ultimately, this more tempered approach seems to permeate Landemore's response to the criticism that it is difficult to ascertain whether a decision is good or not at the moment it is made: 'In the here and now, at time T—the time of the decision—your only alternative is to involve one, few, or many people in the decision procedure. All I'm saying is that at time T you'll likely better off with the decision that involves the greatest number of people.' (Knight et al. 2016, 146). In this nuanced account, the focus is now placed on the mechanisms of aggregation of preferences and, particularly, on exploring the conditions under which hypotheses such as 'more is smarter' (Landemore 2012a, 265) or 'it is often better to have a group of cognitively diverse people than a group of very smart people who think alike' (Landemore 2012a, 260) can be successfully tested.

2.3.1 Some Mechanisms of Aggregation in Epistemic Approaches

The epistemic-democratic literature explores a number of mechanisms that can support the argument for the epistemic properties of aggregation. The most popular are the Condorcet Jury Theorem (CJT) and its different variants and, most recently, the 'miracle of aggregation' (e.g. Converse 1990; Surowiecki 2004), and the Diversity Trumps Ability (DTA) theorem by Hong and Page (2004). Let's briefly review the three of them.

The Jury Theorem proposed by Condorcet in 1785 draws from the law of large numbers and applies to issues that offer only two options, with one correct answer. There are a number of variants of the CJT, including a generalisation of the theorem from majority voting over two options to plurality voting over many options (List and Goodin 2001). As Landemore presents it in its standard formulation, the majority of voters will be "virtually certain to track the 'truth'" if three conditions are met: '(1) voters are better than random at choosing true propositions; (2) they vote independently of each other; and (3) they vote sincerely or truthfully' (Landemore 2012a, 265). The CJT has been largely scrutinised for its 'value for democratic theory'. For example, David Austen-Smith and Jeffrey Banks first

[5]Alternatively, Schwartzberg proposes a more limited, 'deflationary model' that denominates 'judgment democracy': 'Like most epistemic democrats, judgement democrats would agree that individuals' beliefs should derive from deliberation, while emphasizing the value of aggregation as a means of affirming each individual's dignity. (…) In doing so, the judgement model evinces the respect for citizens than epistemic democrats have long displayed. But it does so without the yoke of an implausible an unachievable independent standard.' (Schwartzberg 2015, 201).

questioned the assumption of voters' sincerity as in a number of models since voting failed to be informative and rational; instead, they suggested that 'the appropriate approach to problems of information aggregation is through game theory and mechanism design, not statistics' (Austen-Smith and Banks 1996, 44). Also using a formal demonstration, Franz Dietrich and Kai Spiekermann have contended that the 'asymptotic conclusion' of the CJT (the probability of a correct majority decision converging to one as the group size tends to infinity) is questionable: 'If the asymptotic conclusion applied directly to modern democracies with their large populations, these democracies would be essentially infallible when making decisions between two alternatives by simple majority' (Dietrich and Spiekermann 2013, 88). Dietrich and Spiekermann tackle one of the most significant concerns in the CJT literature—the potential violation of voters' independence via exchange of information and deliberation—and note that it is 'not always obvious whether deliberation overall increases or decreases dependence, another reason why the classical CJT literature struggles so much with deliberation' (Dietrich and Spieckermann 2013, 106). Their proposal consists on a new notion of independence, based on causal networks models, where deliberation not only does not undermine independence but also augments voters' competence: 'Consequently, a group of deliberating economists may perform better because they are more likely to face decisions they tend to get right, while isolated economists may not' (Dietrich and Spieckermann 2013, 106). Whereas this model reconciles deliberation and competence with epistemic arguments for democracy based on jury theorems there is still, as Schwartzberg notes, a lack of systematic testing of these models and thus empirical evidence to demonstrate how judgements are achieved as well as their epistemic value (Schwartzberg 2015, 195–197).

The 'miracle of aggregation' is another application of the 'law of large numbers' evident in different models. A simple explanation is the one offered by Marc Keuschnigg and Christian Ganser: 'the central tendency of a set of independent estimates represents the truth more closely than the typical individual estimation' (Keuschnigg and Ganser 2016, 1). Landemore reviews three versions of this model, which she denominates 'elitist', 'democratic', and 'distributed'. The first version is labeled as 'elitist' as it relies on the presence of 'informed people' in the group to arrive at a 'right answer' and thus is a form of 'elite' extraction. In the second 'democratic' version by Page and Shapiro (1992) no elite has the right answer and everyone is roughly correct (the errors cancel each other and the collective decision is more accurate than the individual guesses). In the 'distributed version', instead, 'the right answer is dispersed in bits and pieces among many people' (Landemore 2012a, 267). The objections that Landemore raises to these 'miracle of aggregation' versions regarding their relevance for democratic theory are twofold: (i) concern about the assumption of independence of individual judgements (as with the CJT); and (ii) empirical defeasibility of the hypothesis of random or symmetrical distribution of errors (Landemore 2012a, 268).

The third mechanism, the 'diversity trumps ability theorem' (DTA) was first formulated by Hong and Page (2004) and later discussed extensively in Page's book The Difference (2007). The DTA model focuses on 'functional diversity' ('differences in how people encode problems and attempt to solve them') and identifies the conditions under which 'when selecting a problem-solving team from a diverse population of intelligent agents, a team of randomly selected agents outperforms a team comprised of the best-performing agents' (Hong and Page 2004, 16386). In other words, 'random collections of intelligent problem solvers can outperform collections of the best individual problem solvers' (Page 2007, 10). The conditions (slightly modified in the 2007 version of the DTA) are that: '(1) The problem must be difficult; (2) the perspectives and heuristics that the problem solvers possess must be diverse; (3) the set of problem solvers from which we choose our collection must be large; and (4) the collection of problem solvers must not be too small' (Page 2007, 10). In a recent replication of the DTA model, Keuschnigg and Ganser have found a particular case where 'ability' remains relevant: 'in determining collective accuracy, diversity is crucial only in large groups and/or in cases of aggregation via averaging. Hence, if forced to plurality vote in a small group—which is often the case in decision-making committees in both firms and public administrations—the electorate must contain highly competent individuals' (Keuschnigg and Ganser 2016, 8). The DTA theorem, nevertheless, has been criticised from different angles. Abigail Thompson has rebutted the mathematical proof provided by Hong and Page and states that, under the proposed conditions, randomness, and not diversity, is what trumps ability (Thompson 2014). In another exposition of the theorem, John Weymark has noted that DTA does not apply in situations involving binary choices and, when there are more than two options to choose from, the assumption about non-strategic behaviour (decision makers sharing information truthfully) may be as questionable as it is with CJT. He concludes by suggesting caution, for DTA 'offers no comfort to those who want to use it to argue for the collective decision to be made by an inclusive set of individuals rather than by an epistocracy' (Weymark 2015, 508).

Landemore considers both the CJT and the 'miracle of aggregation' as accounts or mechanisms of collective intelligence drawing from statistics and probability theory. The DTA theorem, instead, would be a more 'cognitive account' as 'it opens the black box of voters' (Landemore 2012a, 268). However, this categorisation might be slightly confusing for two different reasons, as we will see.

First, although 'account' and 'mechanism' seem to be used indistinctively in her essay, Landemore initially states that "'mechanism' is a loose term by which we mean to refer to the concrete institutions that channel collective wisdom, such as expert committees, deliberative assemblies, deliberative communities like Wikipedia, majority rule, information markets, or the ranking algorithms of search engines such as Google' (Landemore 2012b, 12). However, the examples that Landemore conflates are distinct: expert committees, deliberative assemblies, or deliberative communities are institutions in the sense of groups of individuals following 'action-guiding rules' (Ober 2008a, 8), while majority rule, information/prediction markets, or ranking algorithms are formalised methods, processes, or techniques. The different versions of CJT and 'the miracle of aggregation', therefore, are formal arguments, methods, or techniques to aggregate individual preferences into a collective outcome, but not institutional mechanisms involving real people and both formal and informal *action-guiding rules*. Likewise, the DTA theorem offers a mathematical argument for collective decision making (rather than a cognitive account) and Page himself, in his answer to Thompson's rebuttal, refuses the accusation of misusing mathematics by assuring that 'In my [*Difference*] book, I caution readers to apply mathematical models carefully, highlighting the subtleties of moving from the starkness of mathematical logic to the richness of human interactions' (Page 2015, 10). Very much like mini-publics are regarded as living laboratories to test the theoretical principles of deliberative democracy, epistemic democrats ask for more 'empirical testing [of] the conditions under which groups of ordinary citizens are most likely to produce wise decisions' (Schwartzberg 2015, 197). Yet, none of the two approaches seem to fully acknowledge Page's call to take subtleties into account. In our view, those subtleties translate into the contextual, intermediate level that shapes human decisions and delimits their implementation, that is, the institutional layer of democratic systems. Human interactions within *ad hoc* mini-publics cannot be disconnected from the institutions that create them, set their governing rules, and apply (or not) their carefully deliberated outcomes. Since micro-deliberations do not happen in a vacuum, institutional agendas, policies, goals, expectations, and values are part of the analysis too. The systemic approach calls for an ethnography of the institutions as much as for empirical white-room testing or simulation modelling.

Let us illustrate this point with a real story about randomness and quizzes extracted from Leonard Mlodinow's book *The drunkard's walk: How randomness rules our lives* (Mlodinow 2009). The main character in this story is Marilyn vos Savant, an American columnist and author listed in the Guinness Hall of Fame for having scored the 'World's Highest IQ' when tested as a child. Marilyn vos Savant has also successfully run the *Parade* magazine column 'Ask Marilyn' since 1986, replying to questions posted by readers on a vast number of topics. On September 1990, a reader (inspired by a popular television game show called *Let's Make a Deal*) asked Marilyn:

> Suppose you're on a game show, and you're given the choice of three doors. Behind one door is a car, behind the others, goats. You pick a door, say #1, and the host, who knows what's behind the doors, opens another door, say #3, which has a goat. He says to you, "Do you want to pick door #2?" Is it to your advantage to switch your choice of doors?[6]

When Marilyn replied 'Yes; you should switch. The first door has a 1/3 chance of winning, but the second door has a 2/3 chance' all hell broke loose. Marilyn reported to have received more than 10,000 letters, some 1000 of them from angered PhDs and academics accusing her of 'propagating mathematical illiteracy', inviting her to check 'a standard textbook on probability' or arguing their case with the more succinct '*You are the goat!*' (Crockett 2015). According to Mlodinov, 92% of Americans 'agreed that Marilyn was wrong' (Mlodinov 2009, 44). Yet, she was right, and her response was not only supported by mathematical proof and computer simulations, but with data from the game show: 'those who found

[6]As quoted in http://marilynvossavant.com/game-show-problem/.

themselves in the situation described in the problem and switched their choice won about twice as often as those who did not' (Mlodinov 2009, 55). The reason why Marilyn got it right and proved some of the best and brightest mathematical brains of our time—including Paul Erdős—wrong lies outside Page's 'starkness of mathematical logic'. Rather, it has to be found in the intermediate level of 'action-guiding rules'. The rules of the TV game show entitled the program host to intervene in an initially random process by using his inside knowledge to bias the result, thus violating randomness (idem). None of Marilyn's outraged critics did factor in the contextual rules that altered the abstract conditions of their models.

As Mlodinov puts it, 'to a mathematician a blunder is an issue of embarrassment, but to a gambler it is an issue of livelihood' (Mlodinov 2009, 56). As citizens (and voters) living in polities, we probably keep being a perpetual source of embarrassment to our political philosophers, although we're not in permanent gambling survival mode either. Most of the time, we play predictably by interacting with shared action-guiding rules. In other words, when it comes to real scenarios, either deliberative or not, there is no mathematical logic capable to fully contain the dynamic interplay between people's behaviours and rules and the emergent pragmatic properties of such an interplay. If that is the case, we still need an institutional theory of democracy to explain how collective intelligence emerges from a myriad of micro-interactions and contributes to produce an epistemically advanced form of government.

Second, what does 'collective intelligence' (CI) mean in the epistemic approaches we have reviewed so far? The notion of 'collective intelligence' gained its current popularity with the publication of Pierre Lévy's book *L'intelligence collective* (1997) who defined CI as a 'universally distributed intelligence, constantly enhanced, coordinated in real time, and resulting in the effective mobilization of skills' (Levy 1997, 13). Lévy's premise is that 'no one knows everything, everyone knows something, all knowledge resides in humanity' (Levy 1997, 13–14). This premise resonates with Edward Hutchins' work on socially distributed cognition (Hutchins 1995) and his effort to resituate the focus of cognitive science as a study of 'the social and material organization of cognitive activity' rather than the solitary individual. Other frequently quoted definitions approach CI as 'the capability for a group of individuals to envision a future and reach it in a complex context' (Noubel 2008, 233); 'groups of individuals doing things collectively that seem intelligent' (Malone 2008); or 'the general ability of a group to perform a wide variety of tasks' (Woolley et al. 2010). In a review discussing the recent literature on CI in humans, Juho Salminen highlights the multidisciplinary character of this emergent paradigm and identifies three levels of abstraction: the micro-level (CI as 'a combination of psychological, cognitive and behavioral elements'); the macro-level (CI as a 'statistical phenomenon') and the level of emergence between the two which 'deals with the question of how system behavior on the macro-level emerges from interactions of individuals at the micro-level' (Salminen 2012, 3–5). If we follow this categorisation, most of the epistemic approaches to democracy that draw on the notion of CI use it in the sense of a macro-level 'statistical phenomenon'. Yet, as we have argued, this may exclude the middle level that emerges from individuals interacting with other individuals and rules: institutions. By considering institutions as a key instance of CI, we also expand our notion of 'epistemic' when referring to democratic systems. Thus, by 'epistemic' we do not refer to the properties of aggregation, the majority rule, or to truth-seeking or better-than-something-else mechanisms of CI. Rather, we understand 'epistemic' in the broader sense of knowledge that is openly shared, used, and remixed. In this regard, we heavily rely on the works of Josiah Ober when he explores the connections between democracy and knowledge using classical Athens as a case in point. And we also borrow from Henry Farrell and Cosma Shalizi's outline of what they defined as 'cognitive democracy' (Farrell and Shalizi 2015). We discuss both approaches in the next section.

2.4 Knowledge, Cognition, and Democracy

Josiah Ober's approach to the relationship between democracy and knowledge can be better illustrated by his proposal to revisit its original meaning (Ober 2008b). Ober considers that it is 'reductive' to define democracy as 'the power of the people (...) to decide matters by majority rule' since it makes democracy 'vulnerable to well-known social choice dilemmas, including Downs' rational ignorance and Arrow's impossibility theorem' (Ober 2008b, 3). He then proposes revisiting the concept by returning to the Greek sources of the term and rendering it 'less vulnerable to the problems associated with aggregating diverse preferences by voting' (Ober 2008b, 3). As opposed to other political terms, Ober notes, 'the term demos refers to a collective body' rather than a number (one, a few, or many) (2008b, 4) and "*kratos*', when it is used as a regime-type suffix, becomes power in the sense of strength, enablement, or 'capacity to do things'" (Ober 2008b, 6). *Demokratia*, therefore 'refers to a demos' collective capacity to do things in the public realm, to make things happen' (Ober 2008b, 7). To make things happen in the public realm, Ober argues, 'democratic Athens depended directly and self-consciously on actively deploying the epistemic resources of its citizenry' (Ober 2012, 118), something quite different from our current political practice that 'often treats free citizens as passive subjects by discounting the value of what they know' (Ober 2008a, 1).

Consequently, a definition of democracy as people's 'capacity to do things', not majority rule, raises the major question of how people can mobilise knowledge to do things, or 'how we put knowledge to work' (Ober 2008a, 3). Ober uses the word 'knowledge' rather than 'intelligence' since, drawing from organisational theory, his notion of knowledge covers 'a matrix of experience, expertise, and information' that is possessed by individuals but which is also 'located in social networks and reproduced by institutional processes' (Ober 2012, 119). The advantage of classical Athens, in Ober's view, was to put knowledge in action 'by transforming raw data and unprocessed information into politically valuable knowledge'—which is aligned with the definition of knowledge in Chap. 1 as 'information used to make a better decision'. Politically relevant knowledge consists of 'people's beliefs, capabilities, experience, and information, organized in ways that can be reproduced and shared within and among collectivities'; and it 'conjoins social/interpersonal and technical/expert forms of knowledge that are possessed by the organisation as a whole (in the form of institutionalized processes and formal codes) and by individuals (both explicit and latently)' (Ober 2008a, 91).

As Ober notes, the Athenian processes are 'quite different from core political processes of modern democratic nation-states' (Ober 2008a, 97). Representative democracy or political parties were not part of the Athenian landscape, and voting for candidates seeking public office did not have the weight it has in our democratic systems. Yet, Ober identifies three problems in the organisation of politically valuable knowledge that are very familiar to any contemporary reader: (i) dispersed latent knowledge problem; (ii) unaligned actions problem, (iii) transaction costs problem. The solution to these three problems relies on institutional designs capable to articulate three different institutionalised epistemic processes: aggregation, alignment, and codification (Ober 2008a, 18). The three of them involve both innovation ('generation of new solutions') and learning ('socialisation in routines of proven value') (Ober 2008a, 19) and are defined as follows:

- Aggregation: the process of collecting the right kinds of dispersed knowledge in a timely manner for purposes of decision making.
- Alignment: [the process of] enabling people who prefer similar outcomes to coordinate their actions by reference to shared values and a shared body of common knowledge.
- Codification: the process by which implemented decisions become action-guiding rules capable of influencing future social behavior and interpersonal exchanges. (Ober 2008a, 26–27).

Ober presents knowledge aggregation in a large participatory democracy as a collective action problem where, for any rational individual, the costs of sharing knowledge exceed the potential benefits. To reverse that situation, some conditions must be met. The first one is more of a precondition: access to low-cost communication technologies that keep the burden to share information to a minimum. Second, either material or immaterial incentives (or a combination of both) to share knowledge must be in place. Third, successful aggregation requires an 'epistemic sorting device', that is, filtering mechanisms that are 'context sensitive' and retain valuable knowledge while leaving irrelevant or useless knowledge out (Ober 2008a, 120). As the costs of aggregating knowledge increase with complexity and scale, both coupled and fine-tuned processes of routinisation and innovation are required. Routinisation preserves the stock of knowledge by 'archiving data, establishing standard protocols, and socializing members into 'the way we do things around here'' (idem). As routinisation may also hinder adaptiveness to changing environments, institutions must be able to preserve diversity and the capacity to absorb external knowledge so that they can innovate and stay competitive.

Alignment in participatory democracy is about ‘carrying out plans in the absence of command-and-control mechanisms’ (Ober 2008a, 168). Ober argues that classical Athens used a combination of mechanisms allowing a seamless transition from decision-making to implementation of decisions: (i) informed leader following; (ii) procedural rules following, and (iii) institutional commitments following. Athenian citizens thus managed to align their behaviour by ‘learning a substantial body of common knowledge, following informed leaders, mastering a set of simple procedural rules, and accepting the credibility of others’ precommitments’ (Ober 2008a, 171). Publicity was critical in the process, for it ‘made relevant knowledge commonly available for uptake’ (idem). But so was the legal system. By using a legal case study (a trial for treason in 330 B.C.) Ober highlights how the legal system ‘played a key role in building useful social knowledge and publicizing commitments, but also in regulating the system by offering reasonable safeguards against socially disruptive cascades of accurate following’ (Ober 2008a, 182).

Codification encapsulates the process of bringing social knowledge into statutory, written form. In Athens as in modern societies, Ober argues, codification can be approached as a mechanism to reduce transaction costs in productive exchanges or, following the work of Ronald Coase, making them ‘as frictionless as possible’ (Ober 2008a, 217). Nevertheless, as there are other complementary instruments which also serve that purpose, the epistemic process of codification is expanded to include not just formal rules, but also dispute resolution procedures, standard exchange media (coinage, measures, weights, etc.), open-access facilities (markets, communications, transports, etc.) and third-party rents (e.g. taxes). Codified democratic rules, therefore, aimed at providing predictability to market exchanges but, ultimately, embodied fairness (or the mutually shared guarantee that similar situations would be treated similarly). A codified principle of fairness helped to consolidate ‘a mass/elite social equilibrium’ and made Athenian democracy more resilient to ‘endemic hostility among social classes’.

In describing the three epistemic processes of aggregation, alignment, and codification, Ober emphasises the role of distributed social and technical knowledge as the fertiliser to the ‘flourishing of democratic organisations’ (Ober 2008a, 265) or, as he will later conceptualise, as a key contributor to ‘efflorescence’, defined as ‘increased economic growth accompanied by a sharp uptick in cultural achievement’ (Ober 2015, 2). Democratic processes enabling widely distributed knowledge and the efficient interplay between economic growth and cultural achievement also made citizens willing to become ‘sharers in a democratic culture’ by ‘rationally [choosing] to participate in the productive work of citizenship’ (Ober 2008a, 267).

What are the implications of Ober’s analysis of democracy in classical Athens? The first one is that a more active, engaged citizenship is possible.

> If management of knowledge, distributed among a diverse population through the operation of participatory institutions, helped to promote high performance in the competitive world of classical Greece, there is less reason to assume that the role of the citizen in a modern democracy need be limited to occasionally choosing among competitive elites on the basis of their party affiliation (Ober 2008a, 267–268).

In addition, the Athenian lessons also suggest that adequate mechanisms of coordination do not inevitably require command-and-control structures in place, as technocratic and elitist arguments would presuppose. Emergent models of commons-based production systems and peer-to-peer (P2P) structures of governance as the ones described, among others, by Benkler (2003, 2006), Bollier (2008, 2014) or Kostakis and Bauwens (2014) provide evidence of similar coordinating mechanisms in absence of centralised authorities. In many cases, low-cost communication technologies and information filtering systems do not just mitigate transaction costs, but actually enable transactions to happen. Likewise, they may help to reduce the increased scale issues that Ober points out. Interestingly, Ober's closing remarks acknowledge that 'the full potential of modern information technology for facilitating knowledge aggregation and public action in democratic contexts remains to be explored' (Ober 2008a, 268). In a similar vein, as Henry Farrell and Cosma Shalizi have suggested in their outline of 'cognitive democracy':

> The rise of the Internet makes this an especially good time for experimenting with democratic structures. Democracy is uniquely fitted to help people with highly diverse perspectives come together to solve problems collectively. Democracy can do this better than either markets or hierarchies because it brings these diverse understandings into direct contact with each other, allowing forms of learning that are unlikely either though the price mechanism of markets or the hierarchical arrangements of bureaucracy (Farrell and Shalizi 2015, 211).

Precisely, exploring the potential of some of our state-of-the-art information technologies for democracy is the core aim of this book. In our approach, we consider that linking digital data, information, and knowledge could be one of the mechanisms contributing to a renewed version of knowledge distribution in our contemporary societies. The following chapter will provide some examples and suggestions in this direction.

2.5 Conclusion

This chapter has outlined two mainstream approaches to democratic theory. Despite their differences, both deliberative and epistemic theories of democracy have more common roots and share more normative ideals than their readings might initially suggest. As Jose Luis Marti argues, a defender of deliberative democracy 'cannot actually hold a pure proceduralist conception' while at the same time an 'adequate epistemic conception of deliberative democracy' must combine intrinsic and instrumental principles (Marti 2006, 28). This confluence of procedural principles and deliberative outputs is also traceable in the experimental design of mini-publics or in the cases that Ober selects to illustrate the unfolding of the epistemic processes of aggregation, alignment, and codification in classical Athens.

The 'linked democracy' perspective proposed in this book does not contradict these previous approaches. Rather, it builds on them to develop the foundations for a theory of the meso level, or an institutional theory of democracy in the digital era.

In this attempt, it largely borrows from these two major contributions to propose, in line with Farrell and Shalizi, a 'broader agenda for cross-disciplinary research involving computational scientists and democratic theorists' (Farrell and Shalizi 2015, 212). These borrowings notwithstanding, our linked democracy approach analogy will require an institutional analysis of democracy (or a meso-level analysis): platforms, apps, blockchains, or digital data are just the technology component of an emergent participatory ecosystem. We need to better understand the properties that emerge through the interaction between people, digital tools and data in order to bridge the gap between technology and institutions, since only the latter, if consistently linked, can propagate the knowledge required to enhance civic action and, ultimately, bring *isegoria* (the equal say of every citizen) into the democratic system.

References

Austen-Smith D, Banks JS (1996) Information aggregation, rationality, and the Condorcet jury theorem. Am Polit Sci Rev 90(1):34–45. https://doi.org/10.2307/2082796

Benhabib S (1996) Toward a deliberative model of democratic legitimacy. Democracy and difference: contesting the boundaries of the political. Princeton University Press, Princeton, pp 67–94. https://doi.org/10.1111/j.1467-8675.1994.tb00003.x

Benkler Y (2003) The political economy of commons. Upgrade: Eur J Inform Prof 4(3):6–9

Benkler Y (2006) The wealth of networks: how social production transforms markets and freedom. Yale University Press, Yale

Bollier D (2008) Viral spiral: how the commoners built a digital republic of their own. New Press, New York

Bollier D (2014) Think like a commoner: a short introduction to the life of the commons. New Society Publishers

Bohman J (1996) Public deliberation. Pluralism, complexity and democracy. MIT Press, Boston (MA)

Bohman J (2009) Epistemic value and deliberative democracy. Good Soc 18(2):28–34. https://doi.org/10.1353/gso.0.0079

Böker M, Elstub S (2015) The possibility of critical mini-publics: realpolitik and normative cycles in democratic theory. Representation 51(1):125–144. https://doi.org/10.1080/00344893.2015.1026205

Cohen J (1986) An epistemic conception of democracy. Ethics 97(1):26–38

Converse P (1990) Popular representation and the distribution of information. In: Ferejohn JA, Kuklinski HD (eds) Information and democratic processes. University of Illinois Press, Urbana, pp 369–388

Crockett Z (2015) The time everyone "Corrected" the world's smartest woman. Priceonomics. 19 Feb

Dahl RA (1990[1970]) After the revolution?: authority in a good society. Yale University Press, New Haven

Dahl RA (1989) Democracy and its critics. Yale University Press, New Haven

Dietrich F, Spiekermann K (2013) Epistemic democracy with defensible premises. Econ Philos 29 (01):87–120. https://doi.org/10.1017/S0266267113000096

Dryzek J (1994) Discursive democracy: politics, policy and political science. Cambridge University Press, Cambridge
Dryzek J (2002) Deliberative democracy and beyond: liberals, critics, contestations. Oxford University Press, Oxford
Dryzek J (2006) Deliberative global politics: discourse and democracy in a divided world. Polity, Cambridge
Dryzek J (2010) Foundations and frontiers of deliberative governance. Oxford University Press, Oxford
Dryzek J (2013) The politics of the earth: environmental discourses, 3rd edn. Oxford University Press, Oxford
Dryzek JS, Niemeyer S (2010) Deliberative turns. In: Dryzek J (ed) Foundations and frontiers of deliberative governance. Oxford Scholarship Online, pp 3–17
Elstub S (2014) Mini-publics: issues and cases. In: Elstub S, Mc Laverty P (eds) Deliberative democracy: issues and cases. Edinburgh University Press, Edinburgh, pp 166–188
Elstub S (2015) A genealogy of deliberative democracy. Democratic Theor 2(1):100–117. https://doi.org/10.3167/dt.2015.020107
Estlund D (1993) Making truth safe for democracy. In: Copp D, Hampton J, Roemer JE (eds) The ideas of democracy. Cambridge University Press, Cambridge, pp 71–100
Estlund D (1997) Beyond fairness and deliberation: the epistemic dimension of democratic authority. In: Bohman J, Rehg W (eds) Deliberative democracy. MIT Press, Cambridge
Estlund D (2008) Epistemic approaches to democracy. Episteme: J Soc Epistemol 5(1):1–4
Farrell H, Shalizi CR (2015) Pursuing cognitive democracy. In: Allen D, Light J (eds) From voice to influence: understanding citizenship in a digital age. University of Chicago Press, Chicago, pp 211–231
Fishkin JS (2009) When the people speak: deliberative democracy and public consultation. Oxford University Press, Oxford
Fishkin JS (2011) Deliberative democracy and constitutions. Social philosophy and policy, 28(1), 242–260
Fung A (2003) Survey article: recipes for public spheres: eight institutional design choices and their consequences. J Polit Philos 11(3):338–367
Geissel B, Newton K (eds) (2012) Evaluating democratic innovations: curing the democratic malaise?. Routledge, New York, pp 90–111
Grönlund K, Bächtiger A, Setälä M (eds) (2014) Deliberative mini-publics: involving citizens in the democratic process. ECPR Press, Colchester
Goodin RE, Dryzek JS (2006) Deliberative impacts: the macro-political uptake of mini-publics. Politics Soc 34(2):219–244
Gutmann A, Thompson D (1996) Democracy and disagreement. Belknap Press of Harvard University Press, Cambridge, MA
Habermas J (1985) The theory of communicative action, vol 1. Reason and the rationalization of society. Beacon Press, Boston
Habermas J (1991) The structural transformation of the public sphere: an inquiry into a category of bourgeois society. MIT Press, Cambridge, MA
Hong L, Page S (2004) Groups of diverse problem solvers can outperform groups of high-ability problem solvers. Proc Natl Acad Sci 101(46):16385–16389. https://doi.org/10.1073/pnas.0403723101
Hutchins E (1995) Cognition in the wild. MIT press, Massachussetts
Keuschnigg M, Ganser C (2016) Crowd wisdom relies on agents' ability in small groups with a voting aggregation rule. Manage Sci 1–11
Knight J, Landemore H, Urbinati N, Viehoff D (2016) Roundtable on epistemic democracy and its critics. Crit Rev 28(2):137–170
Kock C (2014) Aristotle on deliberation. In: Van Belle H, Rutten K, Gillaerts P, Van De Mieroop D, Van Gorp B (eds) Let's talk politics: new essays on deliberative rhetoric, vol 6. John Benjamins Publishing Company, pp 13–25

Kostakis V, Bauwens M (2014) Network society and future scenarios for a collaborative economy. Springer, Heidelberg. https://doi.org/10.1057/9781137406897

Kuyper J (2015) Democratic deliberation in the modern world: the systemic turn. Crit Rev 27 (1):49–63

Lafont C (2015) Deliberation, participation, and democratic legitimacy: should deliberative mini-publics shape public policy? J Polit Philos 23(1):40–63

Landemore H (2012a) Democratic reason: the mechanisms of collective intelligence in politics. In: Landemore H, Elster J (eds) Collective wisdom: principles and mechanisms. Cambridge University Press, Cambridge

Landemore H (2012b) Collective wisdom: old and new. In: Landemore H, Elster J (eds) Collective wisdom: principles and mechanisms. Cambridge University Press, Cambridge

Landemore H (2013) Democratic reason: politics, collective intelligence, and the rule of the many. Princeton University Press, Princeton

Lee CW (2015) Do-it-yourself democracy. The rise of public-engagement industry. Oxford University Press, Oxford

Lévy P (1997) Collective intelligence: mankind's emerging world in cyberspace, trans. Robert Bononno. Perseus, Cambridge, Mass

Levy R (2013) The law of deliberative democracy: seeding the field. Election Law J Rules Polit Policy 12(4):355–371. https://doi.org/10.1089/elj.2013.1242

List C, Goodin RE (2001) Epistemic democracy: generalizing the Condorcet jury theorem. J Polit Philos 9(3):277–306

Malone TW (2008) What is collective intelligence and what will we do about it. Collective intelligence: creating a prosperous world at peace. Earth Intelligence Network, Oakton, Virginia, pp 1–4

Mansbridge J (2010) Deliberative polling as the gold standard. Good Soc 19(1):55–62. https://doi.org/10.5325/goodsociety.19.1.0055

Mansbridge J, Parkinson J (eds) (2012) Deliberative systems: deliberative democracy at the large scale. Cambridge University Press, Cambridge. https://doi.org/10.1017/cbo9781139178914

Mansbridge J, Bohman J, Chambers S, Christiano T, Fung A, Parkinson J, Thompson DF, Warren ME (2012) A systemic approach to deliberative democracy. In: Mansbridge JJ, Parkinson JP (eds) Deliberative systems: deliberative democracy at the large scale. Cambridge University Press, Cambridge, pp 1–26

Marti JL (2006) The epistemic conception of deliberative democracy defended: reasons, rightness, and equal political autonomy. In: Besson S, Martí JL (eds) Deliberative democracy and its discontents. Ashgate Publishing Ltd., Aldershot, UK, pp 27–56

Mlodinow L (2009) The drunkard's walk: how randomness rules our lives. Vintage Books

Noubel JF (2008) Collective intelligence: from pyramidal to global. Collective intelligence: creating a prosperous world at peace. Oakton, Virginia, pp 225–234

Ober J (2008a) Democracy and knowledge: innovation and learning in classical Athens. Princeton University Press, Princeton, NJ

Ober J (2008b) The original meaning of "democracy": capacity to do things, not majority rule. Constellations 15(1):3–9

Ober J (2012) Epistemic democracy in classical Athens. In: Landemore H, Elster J (eds) Collective wisdom: principles and mechanisms. Cambridge University Press, Cambridge, pp 118–146

Ober J (2015) The raise and fall of classical Greece. Princeton University Press, Princeton, NJ

Page BI, Shapiro RY (1992) The rational public: fifty years of trends in Americans' policy preferences. University of Chicago Press, Chicago

Page SE (2007) The difference: how the power of diversity creates better groups, firms, schools, and societies. Princeton University Press, Princeton, NJ

Page SE (2015) Diversity trumps ability and the proper use of mathematics—letter to the editor. Notices AMS 62(1):9–10

Parkinson J (2006) Deliberating in the real world. Oxford University Press, Oxford

Rawls J (1999) A theory of justice. Harvard University Press, Cambridge, MA

Rawls J (2001) The law of people: with "The Idea of Public Reason Revisited". Harvard University Press, Cambridge, MA

Ryan M, Smith G (2014) Defining mini-publics. In: Grönlund K, Bächtiger A, Setälä M (eds) Deliberative mini-publics: involving citizens in the democratic process. ECPR Press, Colchester, UK, pp 9–26

Salminen J (2012) Collective intelligence in humans: a literature review. arXiv preprint arXiv:1204.3401

Sanders L (1997) Against deliberation. Polit Theor 25(3):347–376. https://doi.org/10.1177/0090591797025003002

Sass J, Dryzek JS (2014) Deliberative cultures. Polit Theor 42(1):3–25. https://doi.org/10.1177/0090591713507933

Schwartzberg M (2015) Epistemic democracy and its challenges. Ann Rev Polit Sci (18):187–203. https://doi.org/10.1146/annurev-polisci-110113-121908

Smith G (2012) Deliberative democracy and mini-publics. In: Geissel B, Newton K (eds) Evaluating democratic innovations: curing the democratic malaise?. Routledge, New York, pp 90–111

Surowiecki J (2004) The wisdom of crowds: why the many are smarter than the few and how collective wisdom shapes business, economies, societies and nations. Doubleday, New York

Thompson A (2014) Does diversity trump ability? Notices AMS 61(9). https://doi.org/10.1090/noti1163

Weymark JA (2015) Cognitive diversity, binary decisions, and epistemic democracy. Episteme 12(04):497–511. https://doi.org/10.1017/epi.2015.34

Woolley AW, Chabris CF, Pentland A, Hashmi N, Malone TW (2010) Evidence for a collective intelligence factor in the performance of human groups. Science 330(6004):686–688. https://doi.org/10.1126/science.1193147

Young IM (2000) Inclusion and democracy. Oxford University Press, Oxford

Chapter 3
Multilayered Linked Democracy

An infinite amount of knowledge is waiting to be unearthed.
—Hess and Ostrom (2007)

Abstract Although confidence in democracy to tackle societal problems is falling, new civic participation tools are appearing supported by modern ICT technologies. These tools implicitly assume different views on democracy and citizenship which have not been fully analysed, but their main fault is their isolated operation in non-communicated silos. We can conceive public knowledge, like in Karl Popper's World 3, as distributed and connected in different layers and by different connectors, much as it happens with the information in the web or the data in the linked data cloud. The interaction between people, technology and data is still to be defined before alternative institutions are founded, but the so called linked democracy should rest on different layers of interaction: linked data, linked platforms and linked ecosystems; a robust connectivity between democratic institutions is fundamental in order to enhance the way knowledge circulates and collective decisions are made.

Keywords Linked democracy · Multilayered linked democracy · Linked data · Linked platforms · Linked ecosystems · World 3 · Institutions

3.1 Introduction

Contemporary democracies face growing scepticism about their capacity to manage complex societal problems. Financial crises, inequality and poverty, climate change and armed conflicts routinely test the resilience of our democratic systems. Researchers are predominantly expressing concern about the developments of the last decade. Larry Diamond draws from Freedom House data to argue that we are in a 'mild but protracted democratic recession' since 2006 (Diamond 2015, 144). Roberto Foa and Yascha Mounk analyse World Values Surveys to conclude that citizens in Western democracies have 'become more cynical about the value of

M. Poblet et al., *Linked Democracy*, SpringerBriefs in Law,
https://doi.org/10.1007/978-3-030-13363-4_3

democracy as a political system, less hopeful that anything they do might influence public policy, and more willing to express support for authoritarian alternatives' (Foa and Mounk 2016, 7). John Boik et al. warn that traditional democratic institutions are failing and that 'the versions of democracy attempted by newly democratizing nations have been even less effective' (Boik et al. 2015). Globally, voter turnout—a standard proxy to measure citizens' satisfaction with democratic institutions—has been steadily but consistently declining since the 1960s (IDEA International 2016).

This sceptical outlook coexists with some unprecedented technology trends: by 2020, about 1.7 megabytes of new information will be created every second, for every human being (Forbes 2015); there will be more mobile phone subscriptions than people on the planet and more than 6 billion of these devices will be smartphones (ITU 2015). Digital technologies not only disrupt business models, they now shape the way we access information, knowledge, and increasingly, the way we exercise our rights. In doing so, they also transform civic action and enable new forms of citizenship.

Political science, media and culture studies, and ICT disciplines have already produced a vast literature on civic participation online (e.g., see meta-analysis by Boulianne 2015; Gil de Zúñiga and Shahin 2015; Martin 2014). In contrast, democracy and citizenship studies have largely ignored the cyberspace and its implications for broader theories and practices of democratisation and citizenship (Polat and Pratchett 2014; Isin and Ruppert 2015; Theocharis and Van Deth 2016). Yet, the new venues for civic and political participation enabled by the geomobile revolution find their roots in well-established traditions. Different conceptions of citizenship derived from liberal, republican, deliberative, and epistemic political theories of democracy are now implicitly embedded in a myriad of tools and apps designed to support a number of activities, such as accessing information, monitoring representatives, making petitions and requests, or engaging in deliberation or document drafting. Are these spaces the seeds of an emergent ecosystem where data, information and knowledge will circulate seamlessly across platforms? At the moment, the organic growth of participatory tools looks more as a fragmentary, disjointed, and disconnected multiplicity of digital silos than an interdependent system of entities with different functionalities and complementary strengths.

As new tools for democratic participation continue to populate the cybersphere, they offer potential alternatives for mass participation. At one end of the spectrum there is a scenario of persistently enclosed silos (filter bubbles and echo chambers,[1] in the worst case) that reinforces both atomisation and reverberation. At the other end there is a dynamic ecosystem that leverages data to generate information and mobilise knowledge for coordinated civic action and collective decision making. We call this second alternative 'linked democracy' as digital technology enables

[1]Your Filter Bubble is Destroying Democracy. Wired, Nov. 2016. https://www.wired.com/2016/11/filter-bubble-destroying-democracy/.

multidimensional connections within the ecosystem: data with data; people with data; people with people; people with government, etc.

3.2 Knowledge Discovery: On the Shoulders of World 3 Explorers

In 1986, Don Swanson, Dean of the Graduate Library School at the University of Chicago, coined the term of 'undiscovered public knowledge' to refer to independent fragments of knowledge that 'are logically related but never retrieved, brought together, and interpreted' (Swanson 1986, 103). Swanson considered 'undiscovered public knowledge' to be part of what Karl Popper had conceptualised as 'World 3' in his 1975 book *Objective Knowledge*. Popper, not without cautioning his readers from "taking the words 'world' or 'universe' too seriously" (Popper 1975, 106) used them to refer to three different domains. Hence, World 1 was the world of physical objects or states; World 2 referred to states of consciousness or mental states; World 3, finally, was the world of '*objective contents of thought*' (idem). The contents of Popper's World 3 are vast and ever-growing. Among them, we find scientific knowledge, problems, arguments, poetic thoughts, or works of art. As this universe of human knowledge is continuously expanding, Swanson argues, it can also 'yield genuinely new discoveries' (Swanson 1986, 103). In this sense, his working hypothesis foresees 'vast areas of World 3 not yet discovered solely because of our limited ability to index, organize, and retrieve information' (Swanson 1986, 107). This anticipates contemporary work on informational retrieval and on computational creativity, a branch of Artificial Intelligence exploring 'the use of computers to generate results that would be regarded as creative if produced by humans alone' (Boden 2015, v). In Swanson's view, 'information retrieval is necessarily incomplete, problematic, and therefore of great interest—for it is just this incompleteness that implies the existence of undiscovered public knowledge' (Swanson 1986, 109). Since a 'total exploration of World 3' in search of all information relevant to a theory (or its refutation) will always be unattainable, information retrieval techniques circumvent total exploration 'by assigning each piece of recorded information (or 'document') different 'points of access' or 'searchable attributes' such as title words, index terms, descriptors, subject headings, or classification symbols' (Swanson 1986, 113). In doing so, Swanson acknowledges that 'it is illusory to think that such handles can encode either the meaning or the relevance of a document with respect to all problems or theories to which it is logically related, especially to problems and theories not recognized or formulated at the time the document is created' (idem). Again, Swanson's point about the essential incompleteness and uncertainty of information retrieval is relevant to linked open data. Today's explorers of World 3 have standardised routes to navigate data, but new knowledge that awaits discovery (and most important, application) will remain elusive without the emergence of institutions supporting the processes of aggregation and alignment as described by Josiah Ober (Ober 2008).

Swanson's account of undiscovered public knowledge was based on scientific knowledge (and, more especifically, medical knowledge) but the Web 2.0 and the explosion of user-generated contents makes it possible to extend his notion to other areas. The cybersphere is now a trove of the most varied forms of undiscovered knowledge, including political knowledge that has been produced in a particular context but remains untapped beyond that boundary. Yet, this knowledge could be useful for deliberation and decision-making purposes in another context, provided that it continues to be relevant in the new scenario (e.g. it covers a similar topic, a similar issue or process, etc.). A mass scale deliberation on how to regulate food packaging in Norway, for example, can provide relevant insights for a similar discussion being held in Canada. But how do we discover that? And how do we identify (and translate!) key ideas, issues, or suggestions debated in the Norwegian case? Do we need to read thousands of posts by the order they were posted? From our perspective, making this emergent knowledge available whenever necessary is a key challenge, and one that can only be addressed by combining different strategies at different levels.

3.3 Data, People, Institutional Arrangements

Open data and linked open data are essential resources in a linked democracy approach as they provide both the elementary contents and the connecting architecture. For the sake of clarity, we adopt here the well-established distinction between data, information, and knowledge that is standard in the domains of knowledge management and information systems. Yet, this process is not automatic nor spontaneous. It requires additional arrangements—such as agreements about what type of data are relevant in any particular context, the human computing procedures to work with them and the rules that will guide the overall process.

We consider these arrangements as 'institutional' for they require: (i) multiple, repeated interactions between people, technology, and data, and (ii) guidelines, procedures and rules to coordinate behaviour, execute processes, make decisions, and manage misalignment and conflict. Institutional arrangements can be pre-existent to the design and development of digital tools or they may emerge and evolve with them. If pre-existing, we have established institutions (for example, local councils, state, and national governments) supporting the design and development of a digital tool with a particular purpose—public consultation, deliberation, voting, etc. This can be part of a broader e-government program or strategy. Some parliamentary bodies have also followed that path. An example of this is Wikilegis, one of the participatory platforms created by LabHacker, a technology unit of the Brazilian Parliament that designs and develops digital tools to facilitate online participation of citizens in the early stages of legislative processes (Ferri 2013).[2]

[2]http://labhackercd.net/.

> Where institutional arrangements are not pre-existent, we have emerging movements and organisations building their own tools, procedures, and rules as they grow. A growing body of literature is now exploring the rise of digitally-savvy political parties such as the Pirate Party in some European countries, Podemos in Spain, or the Five Star Movement in Italy (e.g. Postill 2017; Simon et al. 2017; Tormey and Feenstra 2015). A more recent example is DIEM25, launched in February 2016 as pan-European movement for "democratising Europe in general and the European Union institutions in particular" (not a political party but a movement supporting third party candidates in national elections across Europe.[3] DIEM25 relies on both an online platform for transnational coordination and on spontaneous collectives (DSCs) to promote the movement locally.

This can also be illustrated with the case of #BlackLivesMatter, the movement that started in 2012 as a Twitter hashtag to protest against the fatal shooting of African-American Trayvon Martin and the subsequent acquittal of George Zimmerman. The hashtag resurfaced on Twitter in 2014 following the deaths of two other African Americans: Michael Brown in Ferguson, and Eric Garner in New York City. The movement, founded by community activists Alicia Garza, Patrisse Cullors and Opal Tometi now has 37 chapters in the US, one in Canada, and has gained traction with support rallies in cities such as Sydney and Melbourne in Australia. #BlackLivesMatter also defines the movement as 'an online forum intended to build connections between Black people and our allies to fight anti-Black racism, to spark dialogue among Black people, and to facilitate the types of connections necessary to encourage social action and engagement'.[4] One of the offshoots of #BlackLivesMatter is WeTheProtesters.org, which describes itself as a 'hub and a source of information', as well as 'a space for protestors nationwide to access the tools and resources to mobilize and organize'.[5] Among the available sources of information is Mappingpoliceviolence.org,[6] a digital map of police violence in the US, built on top of other Web sources. The mappers deploy different procedures to visualise and locate violent incidents, including aggregation of crowdsourced datasets, social media monitoring, and information retrieval:

> This information has been meticulously sourced from the three largest, most comprehensive and impartial crowdsourced databases on police killings in the country: FatalEncounters.org, the U.S. Police Shootings Database and KilledbyPolice.net. We've also done extensive original research to further improve the quality and completeness of the data; searching social media, obituaries, criminal records databases, police reports and other sources to identify the race of 91% of all victims in the database.[7]

---

[3]https://diem25.org/organising-principles/.

[4]http://blacklivesmatter.com/.

[5]http://www.wetheprotesters.org/exe-sum-and-overview.

[6]http://mappingpoliceviolence.org/.

[7]Idem.

As the civil rights activists put it 'we were able to almost create an alternative institution that did a better job of collecting [data on this issue] than the federal government' (Peters 2016). In a related project that aims to hold police chiefs and mayors accountable for violent incidents,[8] activists also deployed a micro-tasking strategy:

'There's actually no national database of local elected officials, what their districts are, what their contact information is, and that's a huge issue when we're talking about policing, which is predominantly local,' he says. 'So all of those things can be crowdsourced, broken up into manageable tasks that anyone can complete'. People with some specialized skills—attorneys or designers, for example—will be connected with more specialized tasks. (Peters 2016).

#BlackLivesMatter and WeTheProtesters.org evolve fluidly as they attract more participants, release and test new tools, and deploy different procedures to achieve different aims as emergent civil rights movements (raising awareness, monitoring, reporting, campaigning, advocating, etc.). While the aims remain the same as their predecessors in this domain, members of the new movements interact with data and tools in innovative ways, such as leveraging social media, deploying crowdsourcing and microtasking methods, or producing and releasing open data with an intended ripple effect.

These cases certainly deserve a more detailed analysis of the emerging institutional arrangements, but they help to shed light on the claim that our linked democracy approach is multidimensional and pays attention to different layers of connections and connectors, which is another way to refer to the new explorers of digital World(s).

3.4 Connections and Connectors: A Multilayered Linked Democracy

Our linked democracy approach builds on a multilayered ecosystem of connections and connectors. Since both connections and connectors are dynamically related, different analogies are possible. The concept of 'layer', widely used in Web science, is one of them. For example, the Internet is usually visualised as a three-layered architecture (with its three main infrastructural, logical, and social layers). Likewise, the Semantic Web is typically represented as a stack of different technologies and languages, and both platforms and apps are now said to be built 'on top of' open data Fig. 3.1.

Linked democracy could also be represented as a three-layered structure that would include: (i) Linked Open Data (LOD); (ii) Linked Platforms (LP), and (iii) Linked Ecosystems (LE). While "linked' in LOD implies the use of standardised technologies (such as URIs to identify entities, HTTP to retrieve resources

[8]http://www.checkthepolice.org/#review.

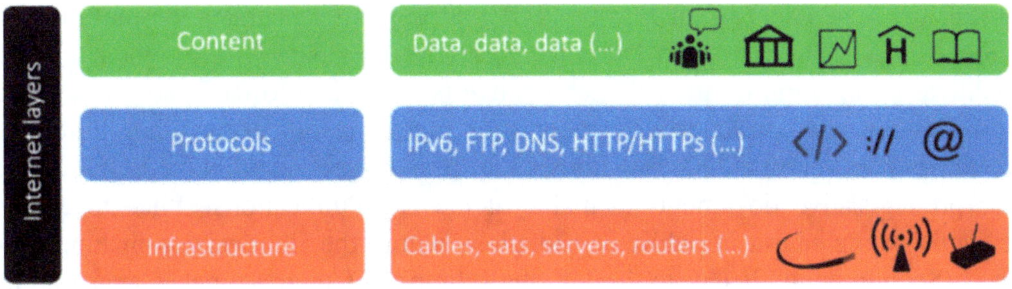

Fig. 3.1 Internet layers

or descriptions of resources, or RDF specifications to structure and connect data that describe things in the world), the concept is not used in the same way in LP and LE, where it refers to loosely connected institutions and ecosystems (and therefore, without the technical infrastructure that characterises LOD). In the remaining pages of this chapter we will present these three layers with more detail. We will argue that the recent developments in LOD are appreciable in many areas, whereas the efforts to link platforms and build linked ecosystems are much less discernible. Yet, a comprehensive linked democracy requires a full-fledged connectome, to borrow the concept that has sparked the mapping of the neural connectivity within the brain (Hagmann 2005). Sebastian Seung, one of the leading researchers in the emerging area of connectomics, defines the connectome as the 'totality of connections between the neurons in a nervous system' (Seung 2012, vii). Our claim is that a robust connectivity between democratic institutions is fundamental to enhance the way knowledge circulates and collective decisions are made. Such connectivity exists and can be mapped now at the data layer, but since our digital platforms remain largely disconnected that knowledge is kept inside silos.

3.4.1 *Linked Open Data (LOD)*

In our approach, the Linked Open Data cloud described in Chap. 1 is a key component of a linked democracy ecosystem. Politically relevant knowledge premised on the LOD cloud is critical for monitoring, deliberating, or making informed decisions. In the last few years, governments, international organisations, and other public and private entities have contributed to the growth of LOD by releasing an increasing number of datasets in LOD formats.

Linked open government data (LOGD) comes with a number of potential benefits, such as 'the reuse of government data, opening up new business opportunities, enhancing government transparency and citizen engagement, and distributing the cost of government data processing to communities' (Ding et al. 2012, 11). The US and the UK portals (Data.gov and Data.gov.uk) and the EU Open Data Portal were among the early adopters of LOGD at the start of this decade and have developed a number of mandates and policies ever since. Other initiatives currently developing in this area are The Talk of Europe (TOE), a project that curates the multilingual proceedings of the European Parliament, enriches this data with biographical and political information on the MPs, and converts these data to RDF, so they can be linked with other parliamentary records or further resources in other European countries (Hollink et al. 2015). Another European project exploits the LOD service for pre-legislative documents available at the EU Publications Office to enable citizens' participation in public consultations within the EU decision-making process (Schmitz et al. 2016). In the US, the Library of Congress makes available its entire collection as a Linked Data Service,[9] and the Department of Veterans Affairs is also using Linked Data 'to integrate over 35 years of health data from over 1200 care sites'[10] (Richards 2015).

The public effort to produce, collect, and make LOD publicly available does not necessarily lead to immediate uptake by other organisations, the private sector, or citizens at large. Although research is still scarce in this area, there are some studies analysing the impact of open data and LOD at the country level. For example, in their review of open data for higher education in South Africa, van Schalkwyk et al. note, 'the open data that are made available by government is inaccessible and rarely used' (van Schalkwyk et al. 2016, 68). To mitigate such 'data viscosity', they argue, intermediaries are essential. As they put it, "intermediaries are found to play several important roles in the ecosystem: (i) they increase the accessibility and utility of data; (ii) they may assume the role of a 'keystone species' in a data ecosystem; and (iii) they have the potential to democratize the impacts and use of open data" (idem). 'Keystone species' in the open data ecosystem are 'actors who bridge institutional boundaries and translate across disciplines, or (…) creators of value in ecosystems by creating platforms, services, tools or technologies that offer solutions to other actors in the ecosystem' (van Schalkwyk et al. 2016, 77). These findings are consistent with another study on UK citizens' perceptions of the usability of open data, which reports that the 'rawness' of open data makes citizens 'unable to use the data for any meaningful purpose relating to their life events or decisions' (Weerakkody et al. 2017). The authors argue that both the advanced analytical skills required to analyse open data and the generic nature of most data repositories are barriers to citizens' use of such data for public policy making debate or decision making. Nevertheless, the different filtering operations required to make data usable for citizens also offer opportunities to develop efficient platforms and interfaces (idem). In his interesting ethnography of the Open Knowledge Foundation in Germany, Stefan Baack observes that 'raw data' typically means 'as collected' and does not imply any 'objective' or 'unbiased' nature (Baack 2015, 4). Baack also notes that the open data community has largely adopted the model of open source projects and communities, and this has an impact on the way they conceive the relation between open data, participation, governance, and democracy:

[9]http://id.loc.gov.

[10]http://vistadataproject.info.

> Taken together, the way [open data] activists apply the open source model of participation to governance results in a notion of a more open and flexible form of representative democracy. 'Open' refers to a higher degree of transparency (by sharing raw data) and the openness of political decision-making processes for public participation. 'Flexible' means that activists think that the inclusion and coordination of citizens' voluntary, 'self-selective participation' should be adapted to the issue at hand and to the local context. (…) From the perspective of democratic theory, they negotiate between representative models of democracy—in which participation is mainly limited to periodic voting—and direct models of democracy, where entire electorates vote on certain proposals. (Baack 2015, 5)

Baack equally points to the key role of 'empowering intermediaries' in nurturing a 'data-driven' paradigm of citizen empowerment (Baack 2015, 6). We refer to these different 'keystone species' or 'empowering intermediaries' as 'connectors', that is, agents whose operations with data and technology enable the creation of more accessible, contextualised, and reusable contents. Connectors have also been referred to as 'infomediaries', or 'intermediate consumers of data (…) [that] play an essential role in making sense of, and creating value out of raw data' (Wessels et al. 2017, 62).

Examples of connectors are journalist networks and organisations that engage in data-driven journalism, such as the Global Investigative Journalism Network (GIJN),[11] ProPublica,[12] Internews,[13] The Intercept,[14] or Bellingcat.[15] In the legislative domain, the platform Digital Democracy makes California and New York state bills, hearings, committees, speakers, and related organisations searchable by keyword, topic, speaker, organization, or date. Videos in the platform are transcribed and can be annotated by its users.[16] Other examples of connectors are Data.world (a social network facilitating collaborative discovery of data), Citygram.org (a platform transforming open data from cities in human readable format), or sites such as Extractafact.org,[17] ResourcesProjects.org,[18] the US Extractive Industries Transparency Initiative, and OpenOil.net[19] (analysing open data from extractive industries). In the area of financial data (budgets, public expenditure, public procurement, etc.) examples include platforms such as OpenSpending.org (tracking and analysing public financial information globally),[20] OpenContracting

[11] https://gijn.org/.

[12] https://www.propublica.org/.

[13] https://www.internews.org/data-journalism.

[14] https://theintercept.com/.

[15] https://www.bellingcat.com/.

[16] https://www.digitaldemocracy.org.

[17] https://www.extractafact.org/.

[18] https://www.resourceprojects.org/.

[19] https://openoil.net/.

[20] https://openspending.org/ (see Höffner et al. 2015).

(publishing government contracting data with the 'Open Contracting Data Standard' and reporting information for different countries),[21] GosZatraty[22] (using Russian public expenditure data to examine, understand and detect abuse or corruption in public procurement), OpenCorporates (an open database with data from about 110 million companies in 115 different jurisdictions)[23] and ProductOpenData (building a public database of product data). Vafopoulos et al. (2016) have recently proposed a top-level ontology (Linked Open Economy (LOE)) to link open economic data. The ontology models the flows in public procurement together with market processes and prices. The LOE ontology, according to its proponents, 'is designed to be a compact common ground established for developers, journalists, professionals and public authorities to use and customize open economic data' (Vafopoulos et al. 2016, 9). As a top-level ontology, LOE could provide 'a baseline to develop new systems, to enable information exchange between systems, to integrate data from heterogeneous sources and to publish open data related to economic activities' (idem).

The role of connectors is also referred in the literature as 'data activism' (Milan and Van der Velden 2016, Schrock 2016). In this perspective, data activism is a distinctive form of digital activism that 'embraces the composite series of sociotechnical practices that, emerging at the fringes of the contemporary activism ecology, interrogate datafication and its socio-political consequences' (Milan and Van der Velden 2016, 3). Data activism can imply different tactics: positive action ('affirmative engagement with data') but also 'resistance to massive data collection' (idem). Schrock's data activism is conflated with advocacy and includes 'requesting, digesting, contributing to, modeling, and contesting data' (Schrock 2016, 581). In Schrock's perspective, data activists are seen as both civic hackers who 'transgress established boundaries of political participation' and 'utopian realists involved in the crafting of algorithmic power and discussing ethics of technology design' (idem). While many open data initiatives may find their practices and rhetorics well rooted in the civic hacking soil, this characterisation entails the risk of leaving a number of other relevant connectors out of the picture. Authors such as Coleman (2013) and Baack (2015) have already emphasised in their studies the heterogeneity of hackers' communities. Especially when it comes to the adoption and further deployment of LOD, the active involvement of governments, international institutions, non-for profit organisations, public and private research funding, etc. makes the landscape significantly more complex than it was a decade ago. The broad range of stakeholders, ultimately, is also an essential component of a linked democracy.

[21] http://www.open-contracting.org/.

[22] https://clearspending.ru/.

[23] https://opencorporates.com/.

3.4.2 Linked Platforms

Since Berners-Lee's first paper on design issues in Linked Data (Berners-Lee 2006), there has been a vast effort over the past decade to build and enlarge LOD infrastructures. Data in the Web are now more linked than ten years ago and the LOD ecosystem is expanding, but silos persist in many areas. Civic engagement technologies are one of them. As John Gastil has written, 'Dozens—and possibly hundreds—of online platforms have been built in the past decade to facilitate specific forms of civic engagement. Unconnected to each other, let alone an integrated system easy for citizens to use, these platforms cannot begin to realize their full potential' (Gastil 2016, 1).

There is no easy solution to this disconnect. The platforms, apps and portals that have proliferated with the advent of the Web 2.0 are usually stand-alone solutions enabling a vast range of civic activities (e.g. signing a petition, voting and/or debating an issue, reporting an issue, following parliamentary activity, etc.). We have elsewhere referred to these tools as crowd-civic systems (McInnis et al. 2017), which can be defined as socio-technical systems blending people, digital technologies, and data for civic engagement purposes: information management, large-scale deliberation, decision making, etc.

Crowd-civic system designers, developers, and users may not explicitly link their digital tools to any conceptual model of democracy and citizenship. Yet, it is possible to connect present crowd-civic systems with different visions of citizenship derived from liberal, republican, deliberative, and epistemic theories of democracy. Highlighting these linkages can help to elucidate the current discussions around 'digital citizenship' that are taking place in a number of academic disciplines (political sciences, sociology, media and communication studies, etc.). As Engin Isin and Evelyn Ruppert have succinctly argued, "any attempt at theorizing 'digital citizens' ought to begin with the historical figure of the citizen before even shifting focus to the digital" (Isin and Ruppert 2015, 19).

Table 3.1 frames a subset of 130 crowd-civic systems (52 of them open source) within different political theories of democracy and their related visions of citizenship. The categorisation of the models (liberal, republican, developmental, and deliberative) draws from previous work by Geoffrey Stokes (2002). We also have added the 'epistemic' model (together with the deliberative one) since some of the crowd-civic systems (e.g. constitution-drafting platforms) combine mass-scale deliberation functionalities with the aggregation of structured ideas, issues, or contents via microtasking (for example, they invite their users not only to discuss the pros and cons of a suggested article, but also to draft a new version of it).

The suggested taxonomy is far from exhaustive. To be sure, an extended survey would certainly help to discover a much larger number of tools currently in use. It is not categorical or clear-cut either, as a number of tools may be linked to more than one model and/or scope. If that is the case, then we consider the core functionality of the tool to determine its most adequate position in the Table 3.1.

Table 3.1 Table of tools and crowd-civic systems

vision	Liberal		Civic/republican / monitorial	Developmental	Deliberative/epistemic	
Scope	Access	Vote	Monitor	Engage/network	Deliberate/design	
	Americadecoded	BallotBin	Abgeordnetenwatch.de	Aavaz.org	All Our Ideas	
	Changepolitics	BoardRoom	Alaveteli.org*	Brigade	Argunet*	Mindhive
	Civi*	Easypolls	Askthem.io*	Change.org	Assembl*	Objective8*
	ClearGov	Electionbuddy	Dailwatch.i.e.	Citizinvestor.com	AvoinMinisterio*	Opentownhall.com
	Congress app	e-Vox*	Del Dicho al Hecho*	Cityflag	Carneades*	Parlement&Citoyens
	DemocraticDashboard	FollowMyVote*	Elections*	Citysourced.com	Civiciti	PolemicTweet*
	DKAN*	Helios Voting*	Elteuparlament.cat	Civinomics	Cohere*	Pol.is*
	Digital Democracy	Horizo State StanVotes	FragDenStaat.de*	Communityplanit. org	Collaboratorium	PyBossa*
	Everypolitician*	OpaVote	GovTrack	Ethelo.org	Common Ground for Action	PopVox
	Followthemoney	OpenVoters*	Issues*	Frankfurt Gestalten*	Compendium*	Reddit
	Intuitive voting	Simply Voting	Nosdeputes.fr*	Fixmystreet.org*	Consider.it	RegulationRoom
	MapIt*	TrustTheVote	Marsad.tn	GlobalCitizen.org	Constitucio.cat	Unanovaconstitucio.cat
	OpenAustralia*	Turbovote	Meinparlament.at	Neighbor.ly	Consul*	Whysaurus.com*
	Opencongress	Vooter	OpenDialog	Neighborland.com	Dastoorikurdistan.org	YourPriorities
	Openstates		OpenParlamento*	OurSay.com	Debate.org	UNU.ai
	PartyofLincoln		OpenPolitici*	Petitions*	Debategraph.org	
	Politicalpartytime		Politikercheck.lu	Represent	DebateHub*	
	Politomix		Pombola*	Seeclickfix.com	Debatepedia.com	
	SayIt*		Questionnezvoselus.org		Debatewise.org	

(continued)

Table 3.1 (continued)

vision	Liberal		Civic/republican / monitorial	Developmental	Deliberative/epistemic	
Scope	Access	Vote	Monitor	Engage/network	Deliberate/design	
	Americadecoded	BallotBin	Abgeordnetenwatch.de	Aavaz.org	All Our Ideas	
	They Vote For You*		Right to Know*		Deliberatorium	
	VoiSieteQui*		Sahana*		DemocracyOS*	
	The Voting App		Theyworkforyou.com*		Discourse*	
	Yoquierosaber		Ushahidi*		EngagementHQ	
	YourNextRepresentative*		Votewatch.eu		LaConstituciondetodos.cl	
			Vouliwatch.gr		Loomio	
			Whatdotheyknow.com*		LiquidFeedback*	
			Writeinpublic.com*		LiteMap*	
			Writetothem.com*		Madison*	

We have followed two basic criteria when including digital tools in Table 3.1. First, we have included civic, grassroots, foundations, research, or start-up initiatives aimed at citizens' participation, as opposed to a number of local, state, and national government-supported consultation platforms (e.g. the ones by states such as South Australia (YourSAy),[24] or by local councils in Mexico City, Barcelona or Madrid (Constitución CDMX,[25] Decidim Barcelona,[26] Decide Madrid[27]), to name a few. Likewise, initiatives by parliaments such as Wikilegis in Brazil,[28] or Mi Senado in Colombia[29] have been left out of our scope. Nevertheless, it is important to note that governments at different levels have currently deployed some of these platforms included in the table. For example, a number of Spanish municipalities, including Barcelona and Madrid, use the open source platform Consul, while some others have opted for Civiciti, which is not open source but offers a free version to small municipalities.

Second, our taxonomy includes tools that leverage some form of crowdsourcing. In this particular context, crowdsourcing methods can consist of outsourcing input information from the general public—e.g. collecting data about candidate representatives and political parties—, collecting ideas, comments, and petitions in a particular area, or designing more elaborated forms of microtasking where participants are requested to complete a specific task—e.g. reporting incidents for election monitoring tasks (with Ushahidi), or providing their version of an article in a proposal for a new legislation, bill, or constitution (e.g. LaConstituciondeTodos.cl or unanovanonstitucio.cat).

These different models of democracy and visions of citizenship (or 'scopes') are synthesized in Table 3.1. Tools marked in with an asterisk in the figure are open source.

A cautionary note is required here, for this synthesis is a highly simplified version of models and conceptualisations that democracy theorists, coming from different philosophical traditions, have been elaborating over the past decades. We are also mindful of Mark Warren's cautioning words: "democratic theorists usually think in terms of "models of democracy"—a strategy that encourages us to center our thinking on an ideal typical feature of democracy, such as deliberation or elections, and then to overextend the claims for that feature (Warren 2017, 39). Our synthesis of models should therefore be read through Warren's lens.

Under a liberal, minimalist vision of citizenship, citizens are basically expected to vote in elections, so that access to information (and limited deliberation) is instrumental to that purpose. Hence, when it comes to the scope of the liberal vision, we

---

[24]https://yoursay.sa.gov.au/.

[25]http://www.cdmx.gob.mx/constitucion.

[26]https://www.decidim.barcelona/.

[27]https://decide.madrid.es/.

[28]http://beta.edemocracia.camara.leg.br/wikilegis/.

[29]http://www.senado.gov.co/historia/item/26548-senado-lanza-app-mi-senado-un-paso-mas-hacia-la-modernidad-y-la-transparencia.

consider these two dimensions: access and vote. 'Access' includes tools that aim at collecting and structuring the data and information that citizens need to know to cast informed votes in political elections. These data can be sourced from open datasets, if available, or crowdsourced from the public. 'Vote' contains those tools whose core functionality (while not necessarily focusing on political processes) is to facilitate the design of and implementation of online elections, polls, or surveys.

Republicanism constitutes a long and rich tradition in political philosophy, inspiring different conceptions of citizenship over time (e.g. Held 2006). From a republican perspective, the protection of the 'public interest' or the 'common good' generally demands greater involvement of citizens in politics, and hence a more proactive role to deter arbitrary abuses of power. As Philip Pettit—one of the main proponents of contemporary 'civic republicanism'—summarised, the protection of republican freedoms and the common interest relies 'on the existence of an active, concerned citizenry who invigilate the exercise of government power, challenge its abuses and seek office where necessary' (Pettit 2003). In this same vein, Frank Lovett points out that 'through collective political action, citizens can bring instances of domination to public attention; they can support laws and policies that would expand republican freedom; and they can do their part in defending republican institutions when called upon to do so' (Lovett 2017).

This vision also resonates with John Keane's notion of 'monitory democracy', which he defines a as "'post-Westminster' form of democracy in which power-monitoring and power-controlling devices have begun to extend sidewards and downwards through the whole political order' (Keane 2009). The list of monitory bodies is extensive and includes, for example, 'public integrity commissions, judicial activism, local courts, workplace tribunals, consensus conferences, parliaments for minorities, public interest litigation, citizens' juries, citizens' assemblies, independent public inquiries, think-tanks, experts' reports, participatory budgeting, vigils, 'blogging' and other novel forms of media scrutiny' (Keane 2009). Although crowd-civic systems are out of the scope of Keane's work, the tools we list in Table 3.1 under the 'republican' vision are monitorial in Keane's sense: tools that enable citizens to ask questions to their representatives, monitor, report and/or map people and political processes (e.g. elections, parliamentary activity, deployment of policies, etc.).

In the developmental vision of democracy, the proactive role of citizens is not restricted to the political realm. Rather, citizens adopt an expansive, far-reaching commitment to enhance the conditions of their (online and offline) communities. In other words, there is a high expectation that citizens will be able to contribute to the betterment of their polity at any of its levels (local, national, or supranational).

This broader consciousness of community and its collective concerns expands to areas where only very recently the Web 2.0 has enabled citizens' involvement at a large scale (for example disaster management or citizen science[30]). The crowd-civic

[30]For a survey of digital tools and platforms for crowdsourced disaster management, see Poblet et al. (2017).

systems considered under this vision aim at engaging citizens to network (e.g. Brigade), participate in detecting community issues and improving the local environment (e.g. CityFlag, CitySourced, FixMyStreet, Neighbor.ly, SeeClickFix) or in supporting both local and global petitions and campaigns (e.g. Aavaz.org, Change.org, GlobalCitizen.org).

Deliberative democrats situate deliberation as the underpinning principle of their theories. Although an ocean of literature has provided multiple definitions and principles over the past two decades, John Dryzek and Simon Niemeyer (2010) have outlined what they consider to be the essential components that constitute deliberative systems. Thus, deliberation is supposed to be: (i) authentic (debate, discussion, or dialogue in non-coercive ways, encouraging reflection and accommodation of diverse views; (ii) inclusive (all 'affected actors' may participate), and (iii): consequential (can determine outcomes such as laws, policies and decisions). Public deliberation by 'free and equal' citizens provides legitimation for political decision-making, therefore, justifications for proposed decisions, policies and law s need to be publicly given and debated to inform the voting public.

Epistemic models have developed in parallel to these visions and the body of literature is not less impressive. Melissa Schwartzberg (2015, 187-88) contends that 'epistemic democracy does not position itself as an alternative to deliberative democracy but instead generally resituates deliberation as being instrumental to meet the aim of good, or correct, decision making'. Similarly, Hélène Landemore argues that 'epistemic democracy is both a subset of deliberative democracy and goes beyond it because it includes things that deliberative democracy doesn't necessarily include' (Knight et al. 2016, 142).[31] According to Landemore, the epistemic models aim 'to emphasize the knowledge-producing properties of democratic institutions and procedures' (Knight et al. 2016, 141). An epistemic vision of democracy, therefore, is consistent with citizens playing an active role in producing contextually relevant knowledge in collaborative ways (e.g. making proposals, drafting of legal texts, etc.).

From this perspective, crowd-civic systems in the last column of Table 3.1 enable the emergence of collective knowledge about topics under discussion. By leveraging different design features that facilitate interaction, debate, and content creation, these systems aim at overcoming the limits of mainstream social media as flagged by a number of studies (e.g. Gürkan et al. 2010; Klein 2015; Iandoli et al. 2016; 2017). For example, as Mark Klein (2015) has aptly pointed out, social media predominance of time-centric discussions (where contents are organised based on

[31]Elsewhere, Landemore argues that epistemic approaches in both democratic and decision-making theory have an extensive genealogy that is evident in argumentation 'running from Aristotle to Dewey… in a deliberative direction'. Acknowledging the selective nature of her exercise, Landemore cites examples from a divergence of theorists from Aristotle, Machiavelli, Spinoza, Rousseau, etc. to make the 'epistemic case for democracy' constructing a linkage to contemporary theory regarding 'collective intelligence' (2013, passim).

the time they are posted) tend to produce low signal-to-noise ratios, insular ideation, balkanisation, non-comprehensive coverage, etc. that may hinder functional deliberation.

To address these issues, a number of crowd-civic systems have incorporated the alternative designs to time-centric systems that Klein (2015) identifies: (i) question-centric systems (Pol.is, UNU.ai) (ii) topic-centric systems (e.g. All Our Ideas, Cohere); (iii) debate-centric (e.g. Consider.it, Common Ground for Action, DebateGraph, Debatepedia); (iv) argument-centric systems, (e.g. Argunet, Carneades, Deliberatorium, Whysaurus). In addition to that, we can also refer to some systems as 'microtask-centric', as they invite users to complete a task (PyBossa) or draft/amend a small text (e.g. Dastoorikurdistan.org, LaConstitutiondeTodos.cl, Unanovaconstitucio.cat). Some tools are also 'internally sequential', that is, they provide a voting system once the deliberation phase concludes (e.g. Assembl, Consul, Civiciti, DemocracyOS). Whether they are also externally 'sequential' in Dryzek and Niemeyer's sense (determining outcomes such as laws, policies and decisions) (Dryzek and Niemeyer 2010), or externally 'aligned' in Josiah Ober's one (facilitating a seamless transition from decision-making to implementation of decisions) (Ober 2008) can only depend on institutional commitments, arrangements, and procedures that are external to the platforms.

Platforms and apps such as the ones in Table 3.1, and more recently blockchain deployments (for example, blockchain-based political parties such as MiVote[32] and Flux[33] in Australia) are just the technology component of an emergent participatory ecosystem. Linked Open Data, as we have seen, is another component, although not necessarily connected to these tools. As Baack puts it, 'even though civic technologies do not always depend on open data, data is key to their functioning in two ways: first, the availability of open data creates more opportunities to develop civic technologies (for example, when they require traffic data); second, they often datafy the activities they are concerned with, i.e. they often create new data' (Baack 2015, 7). Much as this interplay between digital tools and open data is a key condition to increase connectivity across crowd civic platforms, it still falls short of achieving the goal of building a 'civic commons' (Gastil 2016) for the benefit of democratic institutions. Working in this direction would also require building ecosystems where people co-produce and share data and knowledge in particular contexts and for specific decision-making purposes. The examples below may help to shed some light in this direction.

[32]https://www.mivote.org.au/.

[33]https://voteflux.org/.

3.4.3 Linked Ecosystems

In January 2016, the Parliament of Mexico approved a constitutional amendment to grant the capital of the country, Mexico City, the enactment of its first constitution. The Mayor of Mexico City started the constitution-making process by appointing a group of 30 experts (many of them with a legal academic background) to discuss and draft a proposal.[34] In order to open up the drafting process to the citizenry, the City Council made available a collaborative editing tool where citizens were able to provide feedback on the specific topics posted by the drafting group.[35] Moreover, as crowdsourced legal drafting does not typically attract a large number of citizens, this approach was complemented with other participatory strategies, namely a survey and a collaboration with Change.org to collect petitions relevant to the constitutional text (at the closing date of the process, 280,678 people had supported 129 petitions). The Constitution of Mexico City was finally published on 5 February 2017,[36] although at the time of writing the Supreme Court of Mexico is hearing a number of appeals to the constitutional text (with 40 out of 70 articles being challenged) by the federal government, two political parties, and other organisations.[37]

The constitution-making process in Mexico City echoes the one in Iceland five years earlier, when the meetings and workings of a Constitutional Council of 25 individuals (drafted by sortition from a larger pool of citizens) were made publicly available in the Council website for comments via social media and e-mail. It also reminds of the Moroccan constitutional reform of 2011 that engaged more than 200,000 Facebook and Twitter users (although in this case the process was not led by a government or a parliament, but by grass-root activists who had launched the platform reforme.ma to collect popular input on the process). These earlier examples sparked a wave of crowdsourced constitution-making processes across the world (Gluck and Ballou 2014; Deely and Nesh-Nash 2014; Luz et al. 2015) with varied levels of engagement and success.

Compared to previous initiatives, the most recent example of Mexico City takes an interesting approach to participation by acknowledging that citizens may have different motivations, interests, skills, availability, etc. when engaging in participatory processes. As digital tools come with different affordances and functionalities, the repertoire of political participation in democratic societies is broadening rapidly (Theocharis and van Deth 2016). Mexico City residents could chose to attend off-line forums and roundtables, use collaborative editing tools, fill surveys, and propose and sign online petitions. This approach can be seen as a linked participatory ecosystem where participants interact in both offline and online environments, leveraging different tools and co-producing a collective outcome.

---

[34] https://www.constitucion.cdmx.gob.mx/constitucion-cdmx/#grupo-trabajo.

[35] https://www.pubpub.org/pub/constitucioncdmx-principios.

[36] http://www.cdmx.gob.mx/storage/app/uploads/public/589/746/ef5/589746ef5f8cc447475176.pdf.

[37] http://eleconomista.com.mx/sociedad/2017/06/12/debate-publico-constitucion-cdmx.

Strikingly, both the Icelandic and Mexican crowdsourced constitutional drafts had similar fates, coming to a standstill as other institutional bodies were involved. In Iceland, the constitutional text went a bit further than the Mexico City one in the procedural stages. While two-thirds of the voting population approved the text in a referendum in late 2012, it eventually stalled in Parliament. And so it remains, despite the efforts by the Icelandic Pirate Party to renew the approval process.

Presented as a new, unconventional form of political participation, the Icelandic and Mexican processes have not lived up to the early expectations of effectively translating the collected political wisdom of the crowds into law. Why is there such a gap between initial hopes and final outcomes? As both cases show, there is no guarantee that embedding participatory components and digital technologies into the process will eventually have an impact on decision making and, ultimately, will lead to more bottom-up, inclusive decisions. The lessons that can be drawn from such experiments are multiple and involve aspects of political opportunity and trust, institutional design, or experts' involvement (e.g. Valtysson 2014; Landemore 2015; Suteu 2015). Furthermore, as Gianpaolo Baiocchi and Ernesto Ganuza write, 'the literature seldom shines a light on the process of implementing participatory instruments themselves or the conflicts these efforts generate within administrations' (Baiocchi and Ganuza 2017, 14).

Another recent example, the Irish Constitutional Convention (2012-2014) may help to shed some light to this missing link. Like its Northern neighbours in Iceland, Ireland went through intense political turbulence in the immediate aftermath of the economic meltdown of 2008. The general election of 2011 marked the collapse of Fianna Fáil, in a defeat that Michael Marsh et al. (2017, 2) have described as one of the 'largest experienced by a major party in the history of parliamentary democracy', and the subsequent emergence of a large parliamentary coalition eager to adopt a broad reform agenda. In this context, the newly-elected government gave green light to a Constitutional Convention (ICC) that would be tasked to discuss and make recommendations to the national Dáil on eight major issues (such as the voting age, the electoral system, the representation of women in politics or marriage equality). The ICC was composed of 66 randomly selected citizens mixed with 33 self-selected politicians, plus an independent chair. This combination was a notable departure from previous experiences—notably the British Columbia and Ontario citizen assemblies of 2003–2004, which explicitly excluded politicians. The ICC would meet on a series of weekends to deliberate and their members would cast their votes by secret ballot. The Convention plenary meetings were broadcasted live and then archived on the official website,[38] which also enabled submissions from the general public on each particular issue. Twitter users could contribute and follow discussions with the hashtag #ccves (or #MarRef for the topic of marriage equality). Digital technology and social media, as in Iceland, extended the reach of the ICC and amplified the debate among a much larger audience. In the specific case of the referendum on marriage equality, it was finally passed in 2015, through

[38] https://www.constitution.ie/.

heavy social media use coupled with extended global media coverage (Elkink et al. 2016).

At its closing date on early 2014, the Irish Constitutional Convention had produced 41 recommendations and nine reports. In a summary of the status of these outcomes, David Farrell (2016) reported that 17% of proposals had been accepted (and 17% rejected), but 63% remained unresolved. As per the reports, which the government had committed to bring to the Dáil for debate within four months of receipt, he also recounted that 'of the five that were responded to in the Dáil, this was generally in the form of a ministerial statement (in the most recent instance made by a junior minister) crammed into the final hour or so of a Dáil session just before a recess, when many members had already left for their constituencies' (Farrell 2015). Farrell, who had been involved in designing and analysing the process together with other academics from the Political Studies Association of Ireland, concluded that while the Convention and its deliberative method brought a real constitutional change (the inclusion of marriage equality), the overall record was mixed and made 'imperative that tighter guarantees are made to require the government to treat [any future Convention] with a lot more respect than it has treated this one' (Farrell 2016).

Farrell's criticism reveals the tensions that novel participatory mechanisms bring into current representative models of democracy. Tensions between participation, representation, and legitimacy are not easy to resolve and require both incentives and alignment mechanisms. Incentives are critical: why should people commit their weekends to deliberate on recommendations that most likely will end up gathering ministerial dust? Should their advice be given for free? How is this voluntary, sortition-based, unpaid deliberation body going to be regarded by professional, elected, and remunerated politicians? On the other hand, we should not assume that the goals of each institution are aligned, because alignment does not happen spontaneously or by mere goodwill. It requires mechanisms that make sure that decisions made by one institution travel across the ecosystem and are effective included in other decision-making processes. This 'alignment by design', so to speak, is the direction taken by the municipality of Utrecht in the Netherlands with regard to its citizen panels:

> The key feature of this process of political innovation is that citizens were randomly selected to participate, they received remuneration for their participation and they could be regarded as an alternative form of citizen representation. In contrast with many other forms of participation such as citizen panels, the advice was not 'free': local government had committed beforehand to follow this advice and to translate it to an energy policy plan. Our empirical analysis of this case shows that an interplay between idealist and realist logics explains why they are 'accepted' by the institutionalized democratic system." (Meijer et al. 2017, 21)

Another example of 'alignment by design' is vTaiwan, the open consultation process started in Taiwan in December 2014. The consultation process started at the request of one of the ministers of the government to gov0, the Taiwanese civic tech community that had already launched civic participation processes as part of the 2014 Sunflower movement (Hsiao et al. 2018). The consultation process follows a sequence of flexible steps.

> vTaiwan process consists of four successive stages: proposal, opinion, reflection and legislation. There is no strict policy in the vTaiwan process to move from one stage to the next. The transitions between stages are decided by consensus from the vTaiwan community. This open format principle enables meaningful deliberation when all stakeholders are ready and willing to collaborate and iterate on solutions. The methodology of the participant-oriented agenda and rolling correction substantially engages citizens and public servants. (Hsiao et al. 2018, 2)

According to the authors, 'an issue will not move into the vTaiwan process without a government authority being accountable for the issue and a facilitator taking charge of the issue.' (Hsiao et al. 2018, 2) This approach, therefore, aligns stakeholders within the community network with members of the executive willing to champion the issue and activate the institutional mechanisms to take the outcomes of the consultation to the legislative stage. As a result of this process, '26 national issues have been discussed through the vTaiwan open consultation process, and more than 80% have led to decisive government action' (Hsiao et al. 2018, 3)

3.5 Conclusion

The examples considered so far can be depicted as political ecosystems where different actors and institutions exhibit some linkages and levels of connectivity. Nonetheless, we have seen that deploying civic tools for large-scale participation or selecting conventions or panels by sortition does not ensure any real influence on either rule making or policy making unless alignment mechanisms are in place. Moreover, it leaves issues of power and inequality largely untouched. Open data can be celebrated to make governments more transparent and accountable, but it takes more than access to data to remove corrupt ministers from office or effectively prosecute illegal donations to political parties. Likewise, we may choose to run our councils, parliaments and event governments by lottery, but that will not make them less exposed to self-inflicted, inequity-prone policies dictated by financial markets and rating agencies, as Greece, Ireland, Portugal, Spain or Italy—and many other countries before 2008—know very well. Any model of democracy, and ours is not exception, should be aware of the conditions that threaten to turn democratic systems into ill-disguised technocracies or oligarchies.

In the following chapter we will discuss some principles that may help to underpin a linked democracy model. We consider these principles as a place to start an investigation that contributes to a multidisciplinary dialogue on how to strengthen both democratic theory and practice.

References

Baack S (2015) Datafication and empowerment: how the open data movement re-articulates notions of democracy, participation, and journalism. Big Data Soc 2(2) https://doi.org/10.1177/2053951715594634

Baiocchi G, Ganuza E (2017) Popular democracy: the paradox of participation. Stanford University Press, California

Berners-Lee T (2006) Linked data: design issues, http://www.w3.org/DesignIssues/LinkedData

Boden M (2015) How computational creativity began. In: Besold TR, Schorlemmer M, Smaill A (eds) Computational creativity research: towards creative machines. Atlantis Press, v-xiii

Boik J, Fioramonti L, Milante G (2015). Rebooting democracy. Foreign policy. Available at http://foreignpolicy.com/2015/03/16/rebooting-democracy-participatory-reform-capitalism/. 16 Mar 2015

Boulianne S (2015) Social media use and participation: a meta-analysis of current research. Inf Commun Soc. 18(5):524–538

Coleman G (2013) Coding freedom: the ethics and aesthetics of hacking. Princeton University Press, Princeton, NJ

Deely S, Nesh-Nash T (2014) The future of democratic participation: my. con: an online constitution making platform. In: Poblet M, Noriega P, Plaza E (eds) Sintelnet WG5 workshop on crowd intelligence: foundations, methods and practices, 1–15

Diamond L (2015) Facing up to the democratic recession. J Democracy 26(1):141–155. https://doi.org/10.1353/jod.2015.0009

Ding L, Peristeras V, Hausenblas M (2012) Linked open government data. IEEE Comput. Soc. 27 (3):11–15

Dryzek JS, Niemeyer S (2010) Deliberative turns. In: Dryzek J (ed) Foundations and frontiers of deliberative governance. Oxford University Press, NY, pp 3–17

Elkink JA, Farrell DM, Reidy T, Suiter J (2016) Understanding the 2015 marriage referendum in Ireland: context, campaign, and conservative Ireland. Irish Political Studies, 1–21

Farrell D (2015) Constitutional convention 'brand' is in jeopardy, Mar 2016. http://www.irishtimes.com/opinion/david-farrell-constitutional-convention-brand-is-in-jeopardy-1.2142826

Farrell D (2016). Final report card on the government's reactions to the Irish constitutional convention, Jan 2016. https://politicalreform.ie/2016/01/23/final-report-card-on-the-governments-reactions-to-the-irish-constitutional-convention/

Ferri C. (2013) The open parliament in the age of the internet: can the people now collaborate with legislatures in lawmaking?. Brasilia (BR): Câmara dos Deputados, Edições Câmara. Available at http://bd.camara.gov.br/bd/handle/bdcamara/12756

Foa RS, Mounk Y (2016) The democratic disconnect. J Democracy 27(3):5–17

Forbes (2015) Big Data: 20 Mind-boggling facts everyone must read, Forbes magazine http://www.forbes.com/sites/bernardmarr/2015/09/30/big-data-20-mind-boggling-facts-everyone-must-read/

Gastil J (2016) Building a democracy machine: toward an integrated and empowered form of. civic engagement. Ash center for democratic governance and innovation, Penn State University, http://ash.harvard.edu/files/ash/files/democracy_machine.pdf

Gil de Zúñiga H, Shahin S (2015) Social media and their impact on civic participation. In: Gil de Zúñiga H (ed) New technologies and civic engagement: new agendas in communication. Routledge, NY, pp 92–104

Gluck J, Ballou B (2014) New technologies in constitution making. USIP, Washington

Gürkan A, Iandoli L, Klein M, Zollo G (2010) Mediating debate through on-line large-scale argumentation: evidence from the field. Inf Sci 180(19):3686–3702. https://doi.org/10.1016/j.ins.2010.06.011

Hagmann P (2005) From diffusion MRI to brain connectomics: Ph. D. Thesis. Lausanne:Ecole Polytechnique Fédérale de Lausanne

Hess C, Ostrom E (2007) Understanding knowledge as a commons. The MIT Press, Cambridge, MA

Held D (2006) Models of democracy. Polity Press, Cambridge, UK

Höffner K, Martin M, Lehmann J (2015) LinkedSpending: openspending becomes linked open data. Semantic Web 7(1):95–104. https://doi.org/10.3233/SW-150172

Hollink LH, Aggelen, AVA. van, Beunders HB, Kleppe MK, Kemman MK (2015) Talk of Europe—The debates of the European parliament as linked open data. DANS, https://doi.org/10.17026/dans-2xg-umq8

Hsiao Y-T, Lin S-Y, Tang A, Narayanan D, Sarahe C (2018). vTaiwan: An empirical study of open consultation process in Taiwan, http://osf.io/jnq8u

Iandoli L, Quinto I, Spada P, Klein M, Calabretta R (2017) Supporting argumentation in online political debate: evidence from an experiment of collective deliberation. New Media & Society, https://doi.org/10.1177/1461444817691509

Iandoli L, Quinto I, De Liddo A, Buckingham Shum S (2016) On online collaboration and construction of shared knowledge: assessing mediation capability in computer supported argument visualization tools. J Assoc Inf Sci Technol 67(5):1052–1067. https://doi.org/10.1002/asi.23481

Isin EF, Ruppert ES (2015) Being digital citizens. Rowman & Littlefield International, London

Keane J (2009) The life and death of democracy. Simon and Schuster, London

Klein M (2015) A critical review of crowd-scale online deliberation technologies. SSRN Electron J. https://doi.org/10.2139/ssrn.2658811

Knight J, Landemore H, Urbinati N, Viehoff D (2016) Roundtable on epistemic democracy and its critics. Crit Rev 28(2):137–170

Landemore H (2015) Inclusive constitution-making: the Icelandic experiment. J Polit. Philos 23 (2):166–191. https://doi.org/10.1111/jopp.12032

Lovett F (2017) Republicanism, The Stanford encyclopedia of philosophy In: Zalta EN (ed) Spring 2017 edn. https://plato.stanford.edu/archives/spr2017/entries/republicanism

Luz N, Poblet M, Silva N, Novais P (2015) Defining human-machine micro-task workflows for constitution making. In: International conference on group decision and negotiation. Springer International Publishing, 333–344

Marsh M, Farrell DM, McElroy G (eds) (2017) A conservative revolution?: electoral change in twenty-first century Ireland. Oxford University Press, Oxford (UK)

McInnis B, Centivany A, Kim J, Poblet M, Levy K, Leshed G (2017) Crowdsourcing law and policy: a design-thinking approach to crowd-civic systems. In: Companion of the 2017 ACM conference on computer supported cooperative work and social computing, 355–361. https://doi.org/10.1145/3022198.3022656

Martin JA (2014) Mobile media and political participation: defining and developing an emerging field. Mobile Media Commun 2(2):173–195. https://doi.org/10.1177/2050157914520847

Meijer A, Van der Veer R, Faber A, Penning de Vries J (2017) Political innovation as ideal and strategy: the case of aleatoric democracy in the City of Utrecht. Pub Manage Rev. 19(1):20–36. https://doi.org/10.1080/14719037.2016.1200666

Milan S, van der Velden L (2016) The alternative epistemologies of data activism. Digital Cult Soc 2(2). https://doi.org/10.14361/dcs-2016-0205

Ober J (2008) Democracy and knowledge: innovation and learning in classical Athens. Princeton University Press, Princeton

Peter A (2016) Meet the startup building the digital civil rights movement. Fast company, 3 Oct 2016. Available at https://www.fastcoexist.com/3064214/meet-the-startup-building-the-digital-civil-rights-movement

Pettit P (2003) Republicanism, the Stanford encyclopedia of philosophy. In: Zalta EN (ed) Spring 2003 Edn. https://plato.stanford.edu/archives/spr2003/entries/republicanism/

Poblet M, García-Cuesta E, Casanovas P (2017) Crowdsourcing roles, methods and tools for data-intensive disaster management. Inf. Syst. Front: 1–17. https://doi.org/10.1007/s10796-017-9734-6

Polat RK, Pratchett L (2014) Citizenship in the age of the Internet: A comparative analysis of Britain and Turkey. Citizenship Stud 18(1):63–80.

Popper KR (1975) Objective knowledge: an evolutionary approach. Clarendon Press, Oxford

Postill J (2017) The rise of nerd politics. Chicago University Press, Chicago

Richards M (2015) U.S. Government: leading the way to a semantic web of linked open data. Available at https://www.linkedin.com/pulse/semantic-web-coming-age-us-government-data-rafael-richards-md-ms

Schmitz P, Francesconi E, Batouche B, Dombrovschi B, Duy D, Landercy SP, Parisse V (2016) Linked Open data and e-Participation in the EU law-making process. In: International conference on electronic government and the information systems perspective. Springer International Publishing, 79–89

Simon J, Bass T, Boelman V, Mulgan G (2017) Digital Democracy. Nesta, UK

Schrock AR (2016) Civic hacking as data activism and advocacy: a history from publicity to open government data. New Media Soc 18(4):581–599. https://doi.org/10.1177/1461444816629469

Stokes G (2002) Democracy and citizenship. In: Carter A, Stokes G (eds) Democratic theory today. Polity Press, Cambridge, pp 23–51

Suteu S (2015) Constitutional conventions in the digital era: lessons from Iceland and Ireland. BC Int'l Comp L Rev 38:251. https://doi.org/10.2139/ssrn.2511285

Schwartzberg M (2015) Epistemic democracy and its challenges. Annu Rev Polit Sci (18):187–203. https://doi.org/10.1146/annurev-polisci-110113-121908

Swanson DR (1986) Undiscovered public knowledge. Library Quart 56(2):103–118. https://doi.org/10.1086/601720

Tormey S, Feenstra RA (2015) Reinventing the political party in Spain: the case of 15 M and the Spanish mobilisations. Policy Stud 36(6):590–606. https://doi.org/10.1080/01442872.2015.1073243

Theocharis Y, van Deth JW (2016) The continuous expansion of citizen participation: a new taxonomy. Euro Polit Sci Rev. 1–24. https://doi.org/10.1017/s1755773916000230

Vafopoulos MN, Vafeiadis G, Razis G, Anagnostopoulos I, Negkas D, Galanos L (2016) Linked open economy: take full advantage of economic data. SSRN Electron J. https://doi.org/10.2139/ssrn.2732218

Valtysson B (2014) Democracy in disguise: the use of social media in reviewing the Icelandic Constitution. Media Cult Soc 36(1):52–68. https://doi.org/10.1177/0163443713507814

Van Schalkwyk F, Willmers M, McNaughton M (2016) Viscous open data: The roles of intermediaries in an open data ecosystem. Inf Tech for Dev 22(sup1):68–83

Warren ME (2017) A problem-based approach to democratic theory. Am Polit Sci Rev 111(1):39–53. https://doi.org/10.1017/S0003055416000605

Weerakkody V, Irani Z, Kapoor K, Sivarajah U, Dwivedi YK (2017) Open data and its usability: an empirical view from the citizen's perspective. Inf Syst Front 1–16. https://doi.org/10.1007/s10796-016-9679-1

Wessels B, Finn R, Wadhwa K, Sveinsdottir T (2017) Open data and the knowledge society. Amsterdam University Press, Amsterdam

Chapter 4
Towards a Linked Democracy Model

Abstract In this chapter we lay out the properties of participatory ecosystems as linked democracy ecosystems. The goal is to provide a conceptual roadmap that helps us to ground the theoretical foundations for a meso-level, institutional theory of democracy. The identification of the basic properties of a linked democracy eco-system draws from different empirical examples that, to some extent, exhibit some of these properties. We then correlate these properties with Ostrom's design principles for the management of common-pool resources (as generalised to groups cooperating and coordinating to achieve shared goals) to open up the question of how linked democracy ecosystems can be governed.

Keywords Linked democracy · Common-Pool resources

4.1 Introduction

In previous chapters we have suggested that our model of linked democracy can be represented as a three-layered, overlapping structure of Linked Open Data (LOD), linked platforms, and linked ecosystems. A linked democracy model represents the distributed interplay between people, digital technologies, and data (see Fig. 4.1). We have also provided examples of digital platforms and ecosystems that exhibit a certain degree of connectedness by tapping on LOD, on open data, or on crowd-sourced data produced elsewhere.

Breaking silos down is a common, distinctive feature of the examples we have reviewed. But are there any other properties than we can distill from these examples? Moreover, is it possible to turn those properties into design principles that help to orchestrate a linked democracy model? Design principles should guide the implementation of a linked democracy model; they should also capture the institutional arrangements needed to produce aligned decision making in a given domain, either local or global. As we have seen with the Icelandic or Mexico City examples, a lack of institutional endorsement of carefully designed participatory

M. Poblet et al., *Linked Democracy*, SpringerBriefs in Law,
https://doi.org/10.1007/978-3-030-13363-4_4

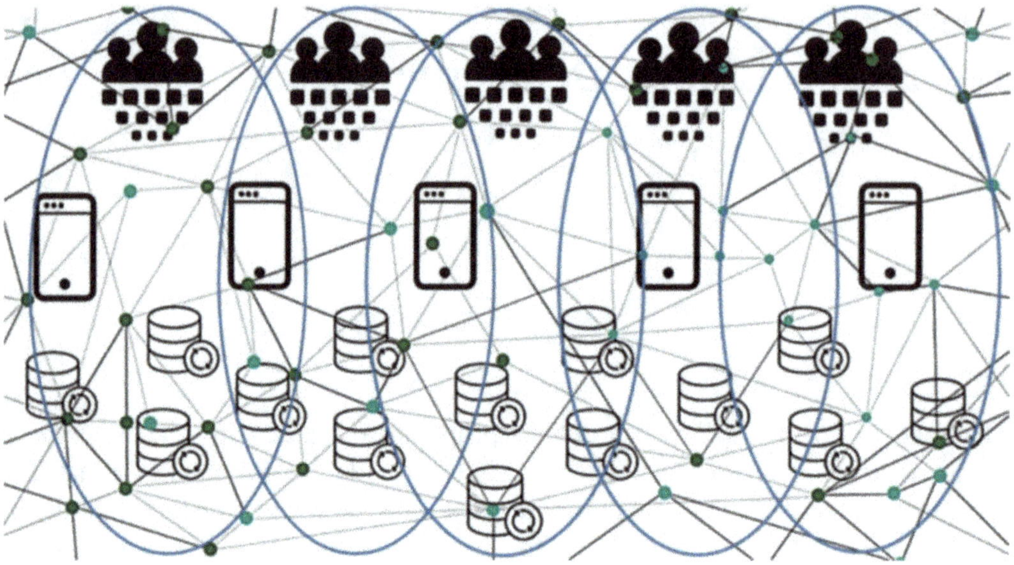

Fig. 4.1 A linked democracy model

outcomes can bring crowdsourced constitutional processes to a deadlock. Linked democracy is about finding ways out of locked democracy.

We are fully aware that generalizing specific design principles for the efficient functioning of a linked democracy would require an exhaustive, large-scale survey of case studies. We have examined some illustrative examples in the previous chapters, but this falls short of providing a comprehensive panorama. Therefore, in this chapter we will first identify some distinctive properties of a linked democracy model based on our previous examples. Second, we will map these properties onto the well-established set of design principles that Elinor Ostrom identified as enabling effective management of 'common-pool resources' (CPR) groups (Ostrom 1990, 90–102). Recently, David Wilson et al. reviewed Ostrom's principles from an evolutionary perspective to argue that they 'have a wider range of application than CPR groups and are relevant to nearly any situation where people must cooperate and coordinate to achieve shared goals' (Wilson et al. 2013, 522). We consider linked democracy ecosystems to be one of those situations involving cooperation—in performing a wide range of tasks—and coordination—of large groups of individuals, so the principles can guide further empirical research in this area. An additional advantage of looking at linked democracy models through these lenses is that the notion of 'politically relevant knowledge' that we have been repeatedly borrowing from Josiah Ober in previous chapters of this book (Ober 2008; 2015) can be also seen as 'knowledge commons', that is, as a shared resource of 'intelligible ideas, information, and data in whatever form in which it is expressed or obtained' (Hess and Ostrom 2007, 7).

Ultimately, the linked democracy model that we propose is partially descriptive. It builds on properties underlined from real examples in politics, law, and policy making. Yet, none of the examples reviewed exhibit all the properties listed below.

Thus, we argue that our model has a prescriptive component, one that helps us to establish some theoretical foundations for what we consider to be a fully operational linked democracy.

4.2 Properties of a Linked Democracy Model

The properties we propose here are distilled from the different participatory scenarios examined throughout the pages of this book. We highlight here the properties that we consider most relevant for analysing participatory ecosystems from the perspective of a linked democracy model. These properties can be described as follows:

(i) *Contextually-bound.* Interactions between people, technologies, and data always occur at specific settings. To borrow Simon's classical concepts, these interactions constitute the 'inner environment' (Simon 1969; 1988) that can be 'represented by a set of given alternatives of action' (Simon 1988, 70). At the same time, people are identifiable as individuals or groups coming together with a common purpose. Depending on the purpose, they may be geographically concentrated or, rather, dispersed across the globe (or both). Either way, people are connected online and the networks they form are traceable; technologies include specific devices and tools (social media platforms, deliberation platforms, participatory apps, distributed protocols, sensors, etc.); data comprises particular datasets with different formats (unstructured data, open data, linked open data, etc.) and licenses of use.

(ii) *Open ended.* Even if contextually bound, participatory ecosystems are also highly dynamic: the interactions between people, technologies, and data evolve and adapt as the context changes, as if in a perpetual beta state. Interests and objectives of individuals, groups, and institutions are not necessarily stable either. A myriad of digital tools are continuously tested; some are adopted widely, some others become niche, and some others are quickly abandoned. As regards data, it is now commonplace to characterise data flows with the 4Vs (volume, velocity, variety, and veracity). The interactions between these three different dimensions are complex, in the sense that the behavior of the ecosystem as a whole cannot be predicted by the behavior of the individual components. If any, a theory of linked democracy is a theory of complex adaptive systems (Holland and Miller 1991).

(iii) *Blended.* Interactions between people take place seamlessly, both offline and online. Global initiatives, or local initiatives that become transnational, may set local chapters where people can meet offline, organise, and discuss (e.g. the European movement DIEM25 or #blacklivesmatter). For Bennet and Segerberg, this hybrid component is a distinctive trait of new models of 'digitally networked action' that leverage digital media as organizing agents (Bennet and Segerberg 2012; 2013). And this is true not just for political initiatives. Massive open online courses (MOOCs) attracting thousands of students across the world typically invite enrolled members to form local groups, organise meetups in physical places and engage in collective learning (Goldberg 2015).

(iv) *Distributed.* Participatory ecosystems can be represented as distributed communication networks with multiple nodes (Baran 1964). The distinction between 'decentralised' and 'distributed' models is not always clear. While the two concepts are often used synonymously, distributed models can also be considered as a subset of decentralised systems (e.g. Eagar 2017). Ultimately, the use of one term or another depends on the choice of a combination of technical specifications—architectural and logical features—and governance models—decision-making processes, regulations, and politics. In our perspective, in distributed participatory ecosystems individuals, groups, and communities can be identified as horizontal nodes, although it is also possible to portray communities as clusters of edges or links. As de Reus et al. have noted, 'link communities have been reported for several empirical networks, including metabolic networks, mobile phone networks and social networks, and have been shown to highlight different subsystems than node-based communities' (de Reus et al. 2014). Such an 'edge-centric perspective' allows for the identification of both 'community hot spots' and redundancies: links from different communities may converge at a single node and a node may belong to more than one single community (idem). This is the perspective currently adopted to map the human 'connectome', a concept first coined by Olaf Sporns and colleagues to refer to 'the comprehensive structural description of the network of elements and connections forming the human brain.' (Sporns et al. 2005). If we extend the analogy to our participatory ecosystems, we can suggest that different participatory ecosystems will exhibit different connectivity maps—or participatory 'connectomes'. Likewise, we will need to develop and refine an appropriate 'connectomics' (Seung 2013) to map and analyse their structuctural connections.

(v) *Technologically agnostic.* Participatory ecosystems rely on tools and technologies that can be replaced at any time. Technologies can fail, become banned, or its supply be interrupted. Nevertheless, it is possible to use, adapt, or develop alternatives in the light of the new conditions. Much as successive bans on Napster and other services did not deter Internet users from sharing files in peer to peer networks, political and civic actors typically find alternative ways to connect and engage in new spaces. The Catalan referendum for independence of 1st October, 2017 offers another interesting example of activists' use of distributed, encrypted technologies to circumvent censorship of pro-referendum websites and to avoid eavesdropping of communications (Poblet 2018).

(vi) *Modular*. Participation and civic engagement are fluid concepts that take multiple forms. Digital tools now support a vast range of options for citizens and groups: data collection, fact checking, monitoring, signing petitions, crowdfunding, ideating, deliberating, drafting, voting, etc. (see Table 3.1 for a taxonomy of these tools). In a modular participatory ecosystem, these options are available to cater for different levels of interest and engagement. Some forms of engagement will likely attract large numbers of participants, while some others, requiring more time, cognitive effort, or dedication, will appeal to smaller crowds. Participation is therefore the combined outcome of modular engagement. The crowdsourcing of the constitution in Mexico City offers an example of designed modular engagement by combining different participatory tools (e.g. a survey tool, a crowdsourcing platform, Change.org, and social media) that target heterogeneous forms of engagement. Likewise, the vTaiwan initiative adopts a modular approach in its four-stage procedure of open consultation, with flexible use of digital tools along the process (Hsiao et al. 2018).

(vii) *Scalable*. Participatory ecosystems should be able to accommodate increasing numbers of nodes (participants, technologies, data) and interactions between them without compromising connectivity and effectiveness. While scalability has many definitions and attributes, from a linked democracy perspective scalability implies an organizational dimension (adding more nodes to the pool of resources); a functional dimension (adding more functionalities); and a geographical dimension (adding more geographical and digital areas and communities).

(viii) *Knowledge-reusing*. Participatory ecosystems tap into collective intelligence to produce new forms of collective, commons-based knowledge. This knowledge may adopt multiple formats: unstructured conversation threads in forums, websites, social media, portals; annotated documents and wiki-documents, crowdsourced legislation and policy drafts, proposals, manifestos, etc.; infographics, reports, case-study repositories, podcasts, videos, etc. Both deliberation and epistemic approaches to democracy assume the need to find and reuse knowledge in deliberation and decision-making processes. Josiah Ober adds to this necessity the dimension of problem solving, in the sense that untapped knowledge can only be 'discovered' in relation to a particular political issue by making a connection of relevance between that knowledge and the issue at hand (Ober 2008; 2015). From a linked democracy approach, we are interested in the potential application of principles and protocols of linked open data to make these connections relevant and possible.

(ix) *Knowledge-archiving*. To reuse politically relevant knowledge, participatory ecosystems need to find ways to trace and reproduce such knowledge. Traceability, reproducibility, and accountability are essential components of collective, commons-based knowledge. This is not different from scientific knowledge. In the last few years, archivists and scientists have renewed their concerns about the importance of keeping provenance and granting reproducibility of research data and research objects in general (not just data, but research protocols, pre-prints, articles, code, software, etc.) (e.g. Corcho et al. 2012). Provenance and reproducibility of scientific knowledge is now supported by the semantic web technologies and standards described in Chap. 1. Taking stock of advances in this area, the idea is that every valuable knowledge product of a participatory ecosystem should be stored along with provenance information, that is, complete metadata information on the authorship, creation date, etc. If a 'research object' now contains everything necessary to reproduce in silicon a scientific experiment, the 'political knowledge object' to be preserved should contain everything necessary to ground every political decision to be made (data about when a decision was made, argumentations, votations, documents produced, etc.). To date, there are only a few examples of knowledge-archiving systems in the space we are considering. Among them, the Manifesto Project, which provides policy positions from over 1000 political parties in 50 countries since 1945;[1] the database Parties and Elections in Europe,[2] which collects data about legislative elections in Europe since 1945; the Constitute Project, a database of nearly 200 constitutions across the world;[3] or Parlgov.org[4] (a database for parties, elections and cabinets for EU and OECD countries). Nevertheless, these initiatives, while providing highly valuable data points, still fall short of elaborating the 'political knowledge object' we are suggesting to be traced, reproduced, reused, and accounted for.

(x) *Aligned*. Participatory ecosystems may emerge bottom-up, as civic engagement initiatives, or top-down, from legislative or open government initiatives. In any case, only if institutional arrangements are in place there will be the consequential decision making and feedback loops that characterise aligned processes. The only example we found of bottom-up initiated, aligned participatory ecosystem is vTaiwan, stemming from the initiative of the Taiwanese civic-tech community (Hsiao et al. 2018). At the other end, there are two cases of top-down generated participatory ecosystems exhibiting alignment: the Irish Citizen's Assembly, whose recommendation of the topic of marriage equality led to a national referendum, and the case of Utrecht's citizens panels, where members are remunerated and the local council commits to incorporate the panels' advice on the policy (Meijer et al. 2017). Perhaps if we had considered cases of participatory budgeting—an institutional innovation from the late 1980s—the results would have been different. Yet, participatory budgeting seems to offer contradictory results.

---

[1] http://manifesto-project.wzb.eu/.

[2] http://www.parties-and-elections.eu/.

[3] https://www.constituteproject.org/.

[4] http://www.parlgov.org/.

> Sónia Gonçalves has identified a trend where Brazilian 'municipalities using participatory budgeting favored an allocation of public expenditures that closely matched popular preferences' (Gonçalves 2014). For Gianpaolo Baiocchi, instead, the relationship between different forms of participatory budgeting and the administration is rather ambiguous: 'If citizens cannot debate and change the rules, if there is no plural inclusion of citizenry, or if decision-making procedures are not transparent, then participatory budgeting may conceal a new form of domination that has nothing to do with a new process of democratization' (Baiocchi 2015, 10).

In Fig. 4.2 below we represent the properties of a linked democracy ecosystem with a graphic model that clusters them in several dimensions.

The linked democracy ecosystem is framed by its specific context, but its boundaries (dotted frame) are open ended and porous, as both the inner and the outer environment evolve dynamically [contextually-bound/open ended]. At the bottom, there is a layer of blended, distributed interactions between people, technologies, and data. On top of this layer, agnostic, scalable and modular technologies can be incorporated from the outer context. By leveraging these technologies, blended and distributed networks produce collective, commons-based knowledge that can be reused and archived with ongoing updates. When decisions are made based on this knowledge, the outcomes are consequential and extend their reach to the outer context, aligning with and informing external processes of decision making.

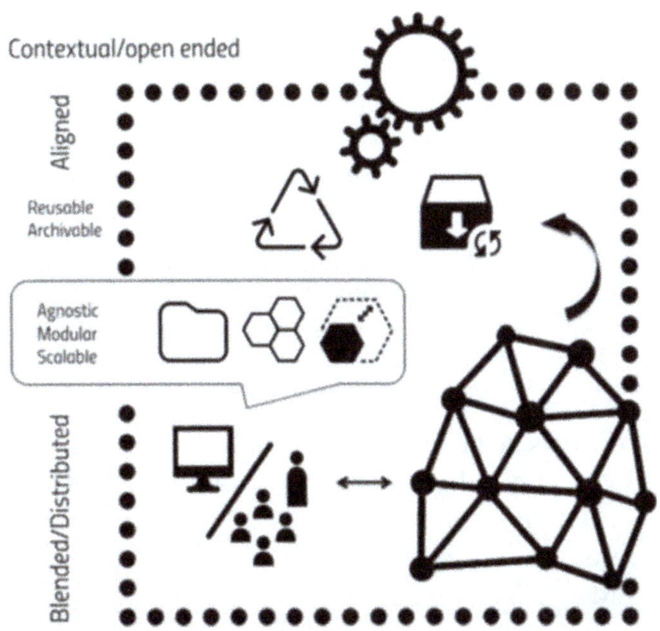

Fig. 4.2 A relational model of properties of a linked democracy ecosystem

4.3 Linked Democracy Ecosystems and Ostrom's Core Design Principles

The properties highlighted above are just conceptual artifacts to capture crucial developments in current participatory ecosystems. These properties do not translate into design principles or institutional rules: we have focused on participatory ecosystems capable of producing collective, politically relevant knowledge, not on how these systems are managed or could be managed. Yet, if we consider linked democracy ecosystems as entities capable of self-managing different forms of commons-based knowledge, we can then check how their properties relate with Ostrom's design principles for the effective management of common pool resource institutions or systems (CPRs). Ostrom's eight design principles have triggered a vast amount of research since they were formulated in 1990. In a nutshell, these principles are (Ostrom 1990, 90):

- Clearly defined boundaries
- Congruence between appropriation and provision rules and local conditions
- Collective-choice arrangements
- Monitoring
- Graduated sanctions
- Conflict-resolution mechanisms
- Minimal recognition of rights to organize
- For large social systems, nested enterprises (appropriation, provision, enforcement, conflict resolution, and governance activities are organized in multiple layers of nested enterprises).

In revisiting this work two decades later, Michael Cox and colleagues contended that 'although there has been substantial support for the principles, some scholars have criticized their theoretical grounding or argued that they are overly precise with respect to the range of conditions to which they might be applied' (Cox et al. 2010: 251). Following their review, Cox et al. proposed a modified version of the principles by splitting three of them in their basic components: in principle 1 they distinguish between 'user boundaries' and 'resource boundaries'; principle 2 is also divided into two basic conditions—'congruence between rules and local conditions' and 'congruence between appropriation and provision rules' and in principle 4 a similar distinction is made between 'monitoring users' and 'monitoring the resource') (idem, 274). A further revision of the principles, as we mentioned earlier, was done by Wilson, Ostrom and Cox, who used an evolutionary framework to extend them beyond CPRs, thus covering many of the situations that involve cooperation and coordination (Wilson et al. 2013, 522).

Both the principles and the analytical framework connected to them are appropriate in the domain we are exploring in this book. In Hess and Ostrom's words:

This framework seems well suited for analysis of resources where new technologies are developing at an extremely rapid pace. New information technologies have redefined knowledge communities; have juggled the traditional world of information users and information providers; have made obsolete many of the existing norms, rules, and laws; and have led to unpredicted outcomes. Institutional change is occurring at every level of the knowledge commons. (Hess and Ostrom 2007, 43).

Figure 4.3 puts the linked democracy (LD) properties next to CPR principles (Ostrom 1990; Cox et al. 2010). Even if they operate at different dimensions (LD properties are features drawn from participatory ecosystems, while CPR design principles are governance principles) there are some relevant connections to underline.

First, LD (i) and (ii) [contextually-bound and open-ended systems] are connected with CPR-P1: they imply boundaries, even if more fluid and porous than the 'clearly defined' ones that Ostrom initially posited. Yet, our LD (i) and (ii) are still congruent with the requirement of a group being able to 'determine its own membership' (Ostrom 2010, 223). Other studies have noted that boundaries are fuzzier rather than rigid in some CPRs (Cox et al. 2010). Ultimately, as Wilson et al. put it, in absence of seemingly clearly defined boundaries, 'the important criterion is for the identity of the group and the parameters of the shared endeavor to be clearly delineated *within each context*" (Wilson et al. 2013, 525).

Second, LD (iii) and (iv) [blended and distributed systems] align with all CRP principles as later work from Ostrom and Hess (2007) includes the online dimension. Moreover, CPR principles (and CPR8 in particular) apply to groups whose governance mechanisms are decentralized, even if the specific implementation may differ from group to group (e.g. polycentric governance, subsidiarity, etc.) (Wilson et al. 2013).

Third, technology-agnostic, scalable and modular properties (LD (v), (vi) and (vii)) are connected to CPR-P2 to P8 as enablers of large-scale coordination and cooperation activities in relation to those principles. In blended ecosystems, issues

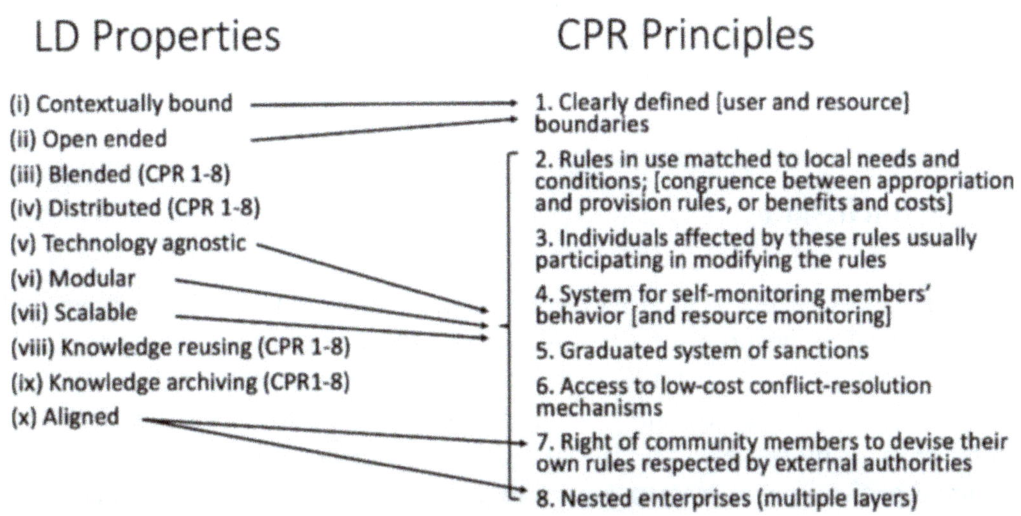

Fig. 4.3 Connections between LD Properties and CPR Principles

of large scale coordination and cooperation become even more complex: for example, how to coordinate a participatory online process to introduce new legislation involving tens or hundreds of thousands of participants?

Fourth, LD (viii) and (ix) properties [knowledge reusing and archiving] can be applied to adjust and fine-tune any of the CPR-Ps to the particular participatory ecosystem. As Wilson et al. note, 'there is a striking correspondence between the principles derived by Ostrom for CPR groups and the conditions that caused us to evolve into such a cooperative species in the first place' (Wilson et al. 2013, 526). Among those conditions, 'our capacity to transmit learned information across generations' (idem, 525). As we have seen in Chap. 1, reusing and archiving are among the core purposes of the Web of Data. For a linked democracy ecosystem, reusing and archiving properties augment our capacity to share and retrieve politically relevant knowledge across and from other ecosystems.

Finally, LD (x) is connected with CPRs P7 and P8. For linked democracy ecosystems to be aligned, it is critical to have internal rules acknowledged and respected in the outer environments (CPR-P7). Likewise, nesting local decision making into multiple layers of governance may help to render those decisions more efficient (CPR-P8). Mansbridge (2014) has shown that these two principles may lead to different interpretations of how Ostrom perceives the role of the state. Thus, Ostrom's alleged 'anti-state' views could be inferred from her wording of CPR-7 ["The rights of appropriators to design their own institutions are not challenged by external government authorities" (1990, 101), cited in Mansbridge 2014, 8]. Yet, Mansbridge also concludes that Ostrom sees the role of the state in many occasions as 'proactive' and she further examines the different functions it accomplishes in managing CPRs (namely, threatening to impose solutions, providing relatively neutral information, offering an arena for negotiation, and helping with monitoring compliance) (Mansbridge 2014).

Our reading of these two principles, to be sure, is neither 'anti-state' nor 'pro-state'. We rather read them with the lens of a linked democracy ecosystem and the collective knowledge it produces. If that knowledge is ignored or distorted, alignment with other layers of governance will not be achieved and the epistemic benefits of democratic participation and engagement will be lost.

4.4 Conclusion

Our goal in this chapter is to provide a conceptual roadmap that helps us to ground the theoretical foundations for a meso-level, institutional theory of democracy. We have mapped the basic properties of a linked democracy ecosystem drawing from different examples that, to some extent, exhibit some of these properties. We then correlate these properties with Ostrom's design principles for the management of common-pool resources (as generalised to groups cooperating and coordinating to achieve shared goals). As Wilson et al. have argued, '[Ostrom] design principles cannot be implemented in a cookie cutter fashion but require a local adaptation to find the best implementations' (Wilson et al. 2013, 527). This approach helps us to raise our next set of questions: how can linked ecosystems be governed? What role does law play? Is a new rule of law emerging from the interplay between people, technology, and data? If so, how does it look like? We try to address these questions in the next chapter.

References

Baran P (1964) On distributed communications networks. IEEE Trans. Commun. Syst. 12(1):1–9. https://doi.org/10.1109/TCOM.1964.1088883

Bennett WL, Segerberg A (2012) The logic of connective action. Inf. Commun. Soc. 15(5):739–768. https://doi.org/10.1080/1369118X.2012.670661

Bennett WL, Segerberg A (2013). The logic of connective action: Digital media and the personalization of contentious politics. Cambridge University Press, Cambridge

Baiocchi G (2015). But Who will speak for the people?: The travel and translation of participatory budgeting. In: November 2010 CommGAP and the World Bank Development Research Group conference on "Deliberation for Development"

Corcho O, Garijo Verdejo D, Belhajjame K, Zhao J, Missier P, Newman D, Palma R, Bechhofer S, García Cuesta E, Gomez-Perez JM, Klyne G (2012) Workflow-centric research objects: First class citizens in scholarly discourse. In: Proceedings of the International 9th Extended Semantic Web Conference. Hersonissos, Crete (Greece), 1–12. available at http://oa.upm.es/20401/

de Reus MA, Saenger VM, Kahn RS, van den Heuvel MP (2014) An edge-centric perspective on the human connectome: link communities in the brain. Phil Trans R Soc B 369 (1653):20130527. https://doi.org/10.1098/rstb.2013.0527

Cox M, Arnold G, Tomás SV (2010) A review of design principles for community-based natural resource management. In: Cole DH, McGinnis MD (eds) Elinor Ostrom and the Bloomington School of Political Economy: Volume 2, Resource Governance. Lexington Books, Lanham, pp 229–280

Eagar M (2017) What is the difference between decentralized and distributed systems? https://medium.com/distributed-economy/what-is-the-difference-between-decentralized-and-distributed-systems-f4190a5c6462. Accessed 4 Nov 2017

Goldberg M (2015) MOOCs and meetups together make for better learning. The Conversation. Available at https://theconversation.com/moocs-and-meetups-together-make-for-better-learning-35891

Gonçalves S (2014) The effects of participatory budgeting on municipal expenditures and infant mortality in Brazil. World Dev 53:94–110. https://doi.org/10.1016/j.worlddev.2013.01.009

Hsiao Y-T, Lin, S-Y, Tang A, Narayanan D, Sarahe C (2018) vTaiwan: An empirical study of open consultation process in Taiwan, osf.io/jnq8u

Hess C, Ostrom E (2007) Introduction: an overview of the knowledge commons. In: Hess C, Ostrom E (eds) Understanding knowledge as a commons. From theory to practice. The MIT Press, Cambridge (MA), pp 3–26

Holland JH, Miller JH (1991) Artificial adaptive agents in economic theory. Am Econ Rev 81 (2):365–370

Mansbridge J (2014) The role of the state in governing the commons. Environ Sci Policy 36:8–10. https://doi.org/10.1016/j.envsci.2013.07.006

Meijer A, Van der Veer R, Faber A, Penning de Vries J (2017) Political innovation as ideal and strategy: the case of aleatoric democracy in the city of Utrecht. Pub. Manage. Rev. 19(1):20–36. https://doi.org/10.1080/14719037.2016.1200666

Ober J (2008) Democracy and knowledge: innovation and learning in classical Athens. Princeton University Press, Princeton

Ober J (2015) The rise and fall of classical Greece. Princeton University Press, Princeton

Ostrom E (1990) Governing the commons: the evolution of institutions for collective action. Cambridge University Press, Cambridge

Ostrom E (2010) Design principles of robust property rights institutions: what have we learned? In: Cole DH, McGinnis MD (eds) Elinor Ostrom and the Bloomington School of Political Economy: Volume 2, Resource Governance. Lexington Books, Lanham, pp 215–247

Poblet M (2018) Distributed, privacy-enhancing technologies in the 2017 Catalan referendum on independence: New tactics and models of participatory democracy. First Monday 23(12). https://doi.org/10.5210/fm.v23i12.9402

Simon H (1969) The sciences of the artificial. MIT Press, Massachusetts

Simon H (1988) The science of design: Creating the artificial. Des Issues 4(1–2):67–82

Sporns O, Tononi G, Kötter R (2005) The human connectome: a structural description of the human brain. PLoS Comput Biol 1(4):e42. https://doi.org/10.1371/journal.pcbi.0010042

Seung S (2013) Connectome: how the brain's wiring makes us who we are. Houghton Mifflin Harcourt, Boston

Wilson DS, Ostrom E, Cox ME (2013) Generalizing the core design principles for the efficacy of groups. J Econ Behav Organ 90:S21–S32

Chapter 5
Legal Linked Data Ecosystems and the Rule of Law

Abstract This chapter introduces the notions of meta-rule of law and socio-legal ecosystems to both foster and regulate linked democracy. It explores the way of stimulating innovative regulations and building a regulatory quadrant for the rule of law. The chapter summarises briefly (i) the notions of responsive, better and smart regulation; (ii) requirements for legal interchange languages (legal interoperability); (iii) and cognitive ecology approaches. It shows how the protections of the substantive rule of law can be embedded into the semantic languages of the web of data and reflects on the conditions that make possible their enactment and implementation as a socio-legal ecosystem. The chapter suggests in the end a reusable multi-levelled meta-model and four notions of legal validity: positive, composite, formal, and ecological.

Keywords Web of data · Socio-legal ecosystem · Rule of law · Meta-rule of law · Semantic languages · Governance · Linked democracy · Semantic web regulatory models · Regulatory quadrant · Legal validity

5.1 Introduction: The Rule of Law in a New Brave World

We will expand in this chapter some ways of implementing linked democracy on legal and political bases. Linked democracy is not only a theoretical approach incorporating open linked data to theories of democracy. It consists of practices and the real behaviour of people exercising their political rights on everyday bases. Thus, it also possesses a personal and cultural dimension that should be valued and protected. Law is an obvious element. Behaviour on the web should be 'fair' and 'legal'. What does it mean? Different states have different jurisdictions, and despite the international trends of the global market, law has been, and still is, dependent on national states.

How could we incorporate regulatory forms of empowering people on the web? How could algorithmic governance, data analytics, and semantics be used to foster the principles of linked democracy that we have just presented at the end of Chap. 4?

M. Poblet et al., *Linked Democracy*, SpringerBriefs in Law,
https://doi.org/10.1007/978-3-030-13363-4_5

We will contend that there are two ways to reach such objectives: (i) embedding the principles of the substantive rule of law into the web of linked data (what we will call the *meta-rule of law*), and (ii) incentivising the creation of *socio-legal ecosystems*, i.e. the social conditions that are required to implement the meta-rule of law online and outline them among all stakeholders and users.

We admit that this can be easier said than done. These two objectives might have an idealistic flavour. A few corporations have a dominant position on the web, they can trade and invade privacy, and they usually do. As Shadbolt and Hampson (2018) have nicely put it, we live in a hyper-complex environment, shaped by our own tools. This is a good breeding ground for elites to thrive. They also point out that "what *has* changed is human potential, thanks to our transformative new tools. [...] The point is not that machines might wrest control from the elites. The problem is that most of us might never be able to wrest control of the machines from the people that occupy the command posts" (Shadbolt and Hampson 2018, 63).

Power is certainly a problem. In our hyper-connected world, we barely know in advance what will come next. But there are protections to be put in place, and rights and duties to be implemented. Some of them differ depending on the country and legal culture. For instance, the common law version of the rule of law is not completely equivalent to its civil law counterpart, more top-down (stepwise) designed, and connected to the structure of the state [*Rechtsstaat, État de droit, Stato de diritto, Estado de derecho*]. There also are striking dissimilarities related to the meaning and the scope of rights (what is meant by the content of rights). For instance, privacy and data protection are considered fundamental rights in Europe, but not in the USA. This affects the level of protection.

Empowering people seems to be the first step to shelter them from democratic erosion. We have drawn in Table 5.1 a raw alignment of the rights and protections of the *substantive* rule of law[1] to the linked democracy properties and principles of Ostrom's Common-Pool Resources (CPR) that we have already introduced at the end of Chap. 4.

This table is what a lawyer is expected to do. Freedom and liberty are pre-conditions for all rights. However, our hyper-connected world is no longer the world we had known before. Enhancing rights and making officers and citizens compliant within a commonly shared regulatory framework constitutes another challenge that we know in advance will not be accomplished in the short run.

Law and Society scholars have highlighted the obstacles that hamper the social and political uptake of the rule of law—the "unrule of law" or "rule by law" in totalitarian regimes, the use of a "regulatory rule of law" as a liberal strategy to contrive a transnational global order, and rule of law abuses in Western states.[2]

---

[1]According to Tamanaha (2004, 2009, 2011) there is a "thin" or "formal" definition of rule of law —set forth in advance, public, general, clear, stable and certain, and applied to everyone according to its terms—and a more substantive one "embracing fundamental rights, democracy, and/or criteria of justice". See also Carothers (1998).

[2]See Ginsburg and Tamir (2008), Gel'man (2004), Uildriks (2010), Cheesman (2015), Merry (2017), Taylor (2017), Abel (2018).

Table 5.1 Alignment of LD properties and CPR Principles with the Rule of Law

Contextually bounded	CPR principles	Rule of law principles
(i) Contextually bounded	1. Clearly defined [user and resource] boundaries	I. Right to assemble
(ii) Open ended	2. Rules in use matched to local needs and conditions; [congruence between appropriation and provision rules, or benefits and costs]	II. Rules in use matched to the protections and boundaries of the rule of law, privacy, and data protection
(iii) Blended	3. Individuals affected by these rules usually participating in modifying the rules	III. Rights of voting and free speech
(iv) Distributed	4. System for self-monitoring members' behaviour [and resource monitoring]	IV. Right of self-regulation; privacy, and data protection
(v) Technology-agnostic	5. Graduated system of sanctions	V. Right of self-regulation; privacy and data protection
(vi) Modular	6. Access to low-cost conflict-resolution mechanisms	VI. Access to justice
(vii) Scalable	7. Right of community members to devise their own rules respected by external authorities	VII. Sovereignty, checks and balance of powers, and free speech
(viii) Knowledge-reusing	8. Nested enterprises (multiple layers)	VIII. Right to education and access to knowledge (innovation); privacy and data protection
(ix) Knowledge-archiving		IX. Right to education and access to knowledge (innovation); privacy and data protection
(x) Aligned		X. Legal compliance

Notwithstanding this, the positive side and protections of the rule of law are deemed to transcend the boundaries of national states to become a general paradigm, an institutional ideal to be embedded into the making of markets, institutions, and human relationships at a global level (Palombella 2009, 2010).

We can assume this ideal, under two conditions. First, we should treat it is as a *design ideal*, not as a fact (i.e. as a series of principles to be nested into the Internet and the Web through the algorithms and the languages of the Web of Data). Second, we should be able to make compatible two competing legal theories of law and regulation operating since the 20th century, namely, formal (jurisprudential)

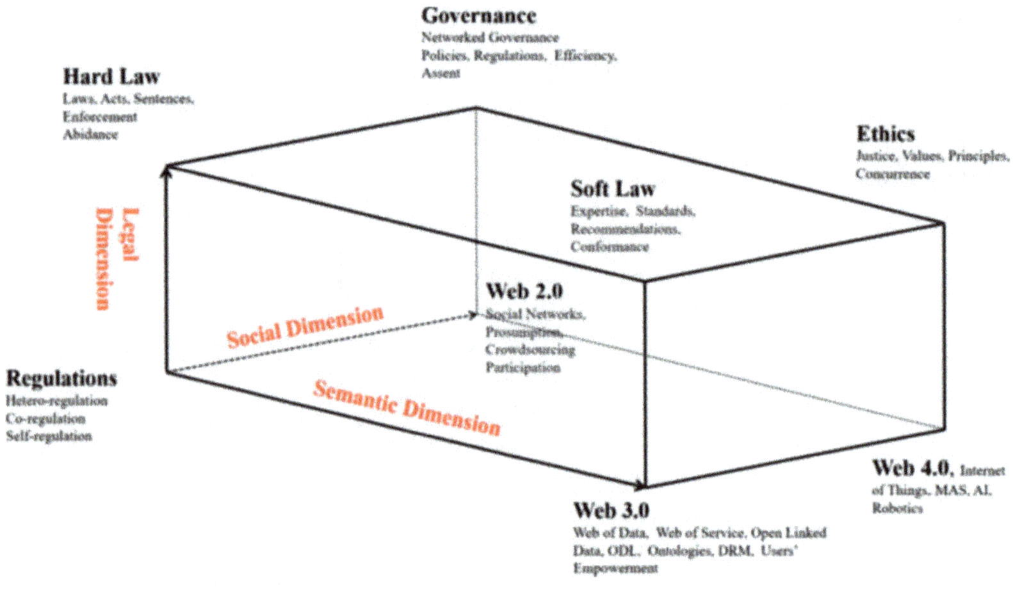

Fig. 5.1 Dimensions of regulatory models

and empirical (sociological) approaches to regulations.[3] This is another ideal that has not yet been completely reached, and whose complexity should not be underestimated.

Figure 5.1 depicts a preliminary general framework in which regulations (including hetero-, co-, and self-regulations) (i) coexist with new instruments of social and political governance on the Web; (ii) are created, implemented and eventually enforced through three regulatory dimensions: legal, social, and linguistic (Web languages); (iii) and are embedded into regulatory models which take into account the "hybrid" interface between human and machines across the Web, the social Web (2.0) and the Web of Data (3.0). It is still preliminary, but the next step seems to be the Intelligent Web (4.0), connecting the Internet of Things, Multi-Agent Systems (MAS), and blockchain technologies with linked and big data—also called *Cyber-physical systems* (CPS) (Xu et al. 2018). It is worth noting that policies, standards and, especially, ethics and values embedded into the systems are expected to play an increasing regulatory role in this new environment. End-users have always been a primordial orientation for semantic web developers (d'Aquin et al. 2008; Domingue et al. 2014).[4]

A few cautionary notes are worth mentioning: (i) the political nature of the rule of law must not be forgotten (the identities and boundaries of individuals, self-constituted social groups, and communities raise different problems of

[3]See on the "new realism" "which aims selfconsciously to theorize the bridge between the world and legal institutions without reducing one to the other", Nourse and Shaffer (2009). See also Selznick (2003), Erlanger et al. (2005), Macauley (2005), Miles and Sunstein (2008).

[4]Cfr. *Re-Coding Black Mirror* Workshops, e.g. Troullinou et al. (2018). See also Taylor and Boniface (2017), EU H2020 Project e-Sides, https://e-sides.eu/e-sides-project.

sovereignty); (ii) principles and values cannot be fully modelled and embedded into computer systems[5] (as the present attempts to code Privacy by Design show)[6]; (iii) the list of legal principles is not exhaustive, and many of them can be combined and applied at every layer of the table (Fig. 5.1); and (iv) there are so many jurisdictions and policies—from constitutional issues to intellectual property, tort law, security and data protection—that it is currently impossible to deal with all specific legal regimes of the web of data at the same time.[7]

Web 3.0—in short, the web of data on the Internet—is constituted by a myriad of languages enacted by the users who produce, use, transform, trade, operate, and interact performing legal and political acts.[8] How might this behaviour be regulated? How can the protections of the meta-rule of law be implemented in this brave new world?

We should first distinguish between *systemic* and *semantic* interoperability. Second, we should consider the insights of cognitive science on how artificial agency and human action can be coordinated to attain collective goals. Third, we should merge legal and political governance, now in separate silos. Fourth, we should re-conceptualise regulatory and legal compliance according to these guidelines. And finally, we could suggest a meta-model bringing all these elements together.

5.2 Governing Linked Democracy: Interoperable and Legal Governance

5.2.1 Semantic and Systemic Interoperability

Semantic interoperability refers to the creation of a common meaning for information exchange across computational systems. Systemic interoperability points at the ability of complex systems to interact, share, and exchange information. The latter focuses on the coordination of practices, including human behaviour, organisational structures, tools, languages, and techniques (Kun et al. 2008; Mathews 2017; Casanovas et al. 2017b). Both dimensions should be analytically distinguished for a co-integration of the computational and social dimensions into the specific ecosystems created through this mutual interface.

---

[5]Cfr. Li (2012), esp. Koops and Leenes (2014), Koops et al. (2016).

[6]See the results of the W3C Workshop on Privacy organised by R. Wennig and S. Kirrane, https://www.w3.org/2018/vocabws/report.html.

[7]We carried out a preliminary analysis for Europe in Rodríguez-Doncel et al. (2016).

[8]The Web 2.0 includes services, platforms and applications, end-users, prosumers (both producers and consumers of information), citizens, and social networks that constitute the grassroots of the new digital neighbourhood. The Web 3.0 includes the methods, languages and computer devices that allow turning content—the information spread over the web—into structured information, that is, into shareable and reusable knowledge.

Computer science and society co-evolve in intertwined ways. From this perspective, we can also distinguish between computational requirements and social (behavioural, organisational) conditions. Computational requirements focus on the description of computationally tractable elements in some language. For example, object-oriented analysis applies object-oriented programming and visual modelling through development lifecycles. Goal-oriented requirements engineering "is concerned with the use of goals for eliciting, elaborating, structuring, specifying, analysing, negotiating, documenting, and modifying requirements" (van Lamsweerde 2001, 2009). Both techniques stress the relationship with end-users and stakeholders to enrich the knowledge acquisition process.

Social conditions imply an empirical description and a theoretical account of social issues, statuses, and conflicts. Turning them into modelling requirements is a non-trivial task of a theoretical nature.[9] It refers to what E. Feingenbaum called "the knowledge acquisition bottleneck" (Feingenbaum 1982), and R. Hoekstra "the knowledge reengineering bottleneck" (Hoekstra 2010). As Hoekstra is suggesting, the rapid increase of linked data poses new challenges for the whole Semantic Web project at the cost of control. Knowledge reuse is more de-contextualised now, and ontology building methodology is becoming more complex as users participate and expert knowledge is diversified, scaling up to more complex forms of cooperation between experts and citizens (Corcho et al. 2015).[10] Citizen science, crowdsourced people's participation in scientific endeavours, is gaining strength and posing more challenges too, i.e. the role that volunteers play in true collaborative co-creation processes at all stages of the scientific design (Celino et al. 2018).

From a democratic perspective, law and legal systems could be shaped in such a way to create incentives for innovation and change. Semantic interoperability between all jurisdictions in national and international legal systems is an important component; the next layer of interoperable laws, as we have shown in previous chapters. But anchoring them into different organisations and social communities poses different types of problems: it requires *systemic* interoperability and new forms of responsive, better and smart regulations to foster citizens' participation and community building. In a big data era, we should not lose sight of how close social bonds are built up:

> [...] we risk overlooking the much more important story here, the *real revolution*, which is the *mass democratisation* of the means of access, storage and processing of data. This story isn't about large organisations running parallel software on tens of thousands of servers, but about more people than ever being able to collaborate effectively around a *distributed* ecosystem of information, an ecosystem of *small data*. (Pollock 2013)

---

[9]See the complete account edited by Motta (2013) on 25 years of knowledge acquisition research.

[10]Their classification (Corcho et al. 2015, 15): (i) upper-level ontology engineers (deep knowledge about formal logic and philosophy); (ii) heavyweight ontology engineers (domain experts); (iii) lightweight ontology engineers (develop vocabularies to be used in the linked data context); (iv) SKOS (Simple Knowledge Organization System) concept scheme developers (interested in developing thesauri and other types of classifications); (v) web developers contributing to Schema.org.

As highlighted in Chaps. 2 and 3, the *meso-level*, the institutional implementation layer that is also required to operationalize linked democracy has not yet been considered in the legal domain. Linked Open Data (LOD) is being implemented, but not Linked Platforms or Linked Ecosystems (LE). The big "connectome" is still the administration. Case law and legislation identifiers, such as the European ECLI and ELI, can be situated on top. There are also serious attempts to link legal multi-lingual resources. CELLAR stores all metadata and digital content managed by EurLex, the EU Publications Office (Francesconi et al. 2015). This is the first step to generate reusable knowledge. For instance, the Law Enforcement Agency Identifiers Crosswalk (LEAIC) is a USA programme addressed to merging crime sources from cities under the county level.[11] It facilitates linking reported crime data with socio-economic data. This does not hail from citizens' organisations, but from government agencies to implement criminal policies. But it facilitates more accurate studies on the use of force by the police (Garner et al. 2018).

The legal domain is a complex one, related to normative and legal theories. There is a top-down drive amongst legal scholars and computer scientists to represent its content as a whole. Thus, the requirements for rule interchange languages presented in Table 5.2 are based on concepts elaborated in normative theory (e.g. defeasibility, validity, and lifecycle of norms). LegalXML, RuleMarkup Language (RuleML), Semantics of Business Vocabulary and Business Rules (SBVR), the Semantic Web Rule Language (SWRL), the Rule Interchange Format (RIF), and the Legal Knowledge Interchange Format (LKIF) are rule interchange languages for the legal domain.[12] Originally, the Rule Interchange Format (RIF) aimed to create a standard for exchanging rules among rule systems. In contrast to other SW standards (such as RDF, OWL and SPARQL) it was clear that a single language would not cover all paradigms for using knowledge in knowledge representation and business modelling (WWW 2013), although the media of exchange between different rule systems is XML.[13]

Gordon et al. (2009) conceptualised ten years ago the main legal components as *requirements* that rule interchange languages needed to comply with. Yet, they also highlighted that there is no language able to satisfy all of them simultaneously. Table 5.2 summarises their results.[14]

This framework was grounded on a positivistic approach, but it addressed new problems and challenged what 'law architecture' or 'legal system' had meant so far, at every layer of the table. Legal drafting, ruling and contracting are still activities carried out through natural languages, and so are legal outcomes. As noticed by Lam et al. (2016), even from this perspective, there are problems with handling the

[11]https://www.icpsr.umich.edu/icpsrweb/ICPSR/studies/35158/datadocumentation.

[12]See Casanovas et al. (2016) for the state of the art for web semantics in the legal domain.

[13]See the WWW RIF Overview (second version, February 2013) at https://www.w3.org/2013/pdf/NOTE-rif-overview-20130205.pdf.

[14]The content of the table is reproduced slightly modified in Balke et al. (2013). The authors explicitly assert that these aspects "contribute to classifying norms and *can be extended to other normative domains besides the law*".

Table 5.2 Requirements for rule interchange languages

1. Isomorphism	A one-to-one correspondence between the rules in the formal model and the units of natural language text which express the rules in the original legal sources
2. Reification	Rules are objects with properties: a) Jurisdiction: limits where the rule is authoritative, and its effects are binding b) Authority: ranking status of the rule within the sources of law (constitutional rule, or statute…) c) Temporal properties: (i) time when the norm has been enacted, (ii) time when the norm can produce legal effects, (iii) time when the normative effects hold
3. Rule semantics	Semantics allows for correctly computing the legal effects that should follow
4. Defeasibility	When the antecedent of a rule is satisfied by the facts of a case, the conclusion of the rule presumably holds, but is not necessarily true). Defeasibility breaks down into: a) Conflicts (rules may lead to incompatible legal effects): (i) one rule is the exception of the other, (ii) rules have different ranking status, (iii) rules have been enacted at different times.[a] b) Exclusionary rules (some rules provide one way to explicitly undercut other rules, namely, to make them inapplicable)
5. Contraposition	If some conclusion of a rule is not true, the rule does not sanction any inferences about the truth of its premises
6. Contributory reasons or factors	It is not always possible to formulate precise rules for aggregating the factors relevant for resolving a legal issue
7. Rule validity	Rules can be or become invalid. Deleting invalid rules is not an option when it is necessary to reason retroactively with rules which were valid at various times over a course of events: (i) the annulment of a norm is usually seen as a kind of repeal which invalidates the norm and removes it from the legal system as if it had never been enacted (the effect of an annulment applies *ex tunc*: annulated norms are prevented from producing any legal effects, also for past events); (ii) an abrogation on the other hand operates *ex nunc* (the rule continues to apply for events which occurred before the rule was abrogated)
8. Legal procedures	Rules regulate also whether or not some action or state complies with other, substantive rules): (i) procedures that regulate methods for detecting violations of the law, (ii) procedures that determine the normative effects triggered by norm violations (reparative or compensatory obligations)
8. Normative effects	Such as obligations, permissions, prohibitions and also more articulated effects) e.g.: a) Evaluative, there is a value to be optimized or an evil to be minimized b) Qualificatory, which ascribe a legal quality to a person or an object c) Definitional, which specify the meaning of a term d) Deontic, which, typically, impose the obligation or confer the permission to do a certain action

(continued)

Table 5.2 (continued)

	e) Potestative, which attribute powers f) Evidentiary, which establish the conclusion to be drawn from certain evidence g) Existential, which indicate the beginning or the termination of the existence of a legal entity h) Norm-concerning effects, which state the modifications of norms (abrogation, repeal, substitution…)
9. Persistence of normative effects	Some normative effects persist over time unless some other and subsequent events terminate them
10. Values	Some values are promoted by the legal rule

Simplified reconstruction, *Source* Gordon et al. (2009)

[a]Accordingly, rule conflicts have been traditionally resolved using principles about use priorities: (i) lex specialis (it gives priority to the mores specific rule), (ii) lex superior (it gives priority to the rule from the higher authority), (iii) lex posterior (it gives priority to the rule enacted later)

deontic effects that are needed in legal practice.[15] For instance, the basic assumption of *legal isomorphism*[16] is meant to bridge the gap between the contents of normative texts and the rules describing them.[17] OASIS standards for LegalXML and LegalRuleML have been based on this isomorphic assumption. OASIS Legal RuleML highlights that "*the legal text is the only legally binding element* [our emphasis] the connection between text and the rule(s) (or fragment of rule) guarantees the provenance, authoritativeness, and authenticity of the rules modelled by the legal knowledge engineer" (Athan et al. 2015). Thus, it embraces legal *hermeneutics* as a fundamental set of privileged techniques to produce legal knowledge (Athan et al. 2014).[18]

This is a convenient assumption, but not generalizable to all possible environments and relationships between subjects, as there is no direct translation from the

[15]RuleML is an XML-based standard language that enables users to use different types of rules (such as derivation rules, facts, queries, integrity constraints, etc.) to represent different kinds of elements according to their needs. However, so far, "it lacks support for the use of deontic concepts, such as obligations, permissions and prohibitions, making it impossible to handle cases with contrary-to-duty (CTD) obligations (or reparational obligations), which is not uncommon in legal contracts."

[16]According to Palmirani et al. (2012) *isomorphism* is "the concept to associate any rule to its provision(s) in order: (1) to have a relationship between rule(s) and legal provision(s) that originated it/them; (2) to have a clear explanation, supported by the original legal text, to provide to the end user as outcome of the legal reasoning process (demonstration). The original legal provision is the only legal binding text; (3) to help the maintenance of the rules knowledge base when the text changes (change management)".

[17]Cfr. Bench-Capon and Coenen (1992), Bench-Capon and Gordon (2009). The authors contend that 'legal isomorphism' has a different function and meaning than the mathematical notion of isomorphism. They are referring to the reflection of legal content into formal languages.

[18]"LegalRuleML endeavours not to account for how different interpretations arise, but to provide a mechanism to record and represent them" (Athan et al. 2014).

content of statutes, codes, directives, regulations and acts, to formal languages.[19] From a linked ecosystem perspective, texts are only a component of the overall social system: in real settings, at the implementing and use level, meaning and cognition are distributed across the ecosystem.[20] In a similar cognitive vein, after their work on MetaLex and LKIF Core, Boer (2009) criticised the bijective mapping of legal rules to logical propositions, and Hoekstra (2009, 161) pointed out that "the need for a language construct, such as n-ary relations should be based on a conscious decision to interpret a use case in a particular way: it is an *ontological commitment*." This is an important epistemic concept that should be made explicit in all modelling of social life, including legal instruments, documents, *and* behaviour of the legal professions.

Other modelling approaches for legal knowledge management are based on a different set of closely related concepts. RELaw Workshops have been held to discuss legal requirements since 2008, including sociological dimensions.[21] However, the essential issue of how to link platforms and ecosystems is still at a preliminary stage.

There are several ways to include stakeholders into the design process, depending on the objectives of the system. Most of legal management systems are compliance-oriented, as the design is mindful of the features of legal knowledge as it is used and interpreted by lawyers, external auditors, and business analysts. They are not primarily intended to comprehend citizens' political participation, nor the features of crowd-civic systems that facilitate interaction, debate, and content creation (referred in Chap. 3, 3.4.2, Table 3.1).[22] However, it has not been ruled out that they could incorporate these functions in the future, as they endorse flexible normative interpretations and end-users' participation, two of the main qualities of relational law. As we will see later, we understand *relational law* as the assignment, embodiment and realization of rights within a shared ecosystem; i.e. creating an aggregated value to foster trust and security in the connection between Web 2.0 and Web 3.0 (Casanovas 2013).

---

[19]See Wyner and Governatori (2013) about the challenges to be faced.

[20]See Hutchins (1995, 2006): "The meaning of a complex emerges from the interactions among the modalities that include the body as well as material objects present in the environment. The effects of these interactions are generally not simply additive. Such a meaning complex may be built up incrementally or produced more or less whole, depending on the nature of the components and the relations among them."

[21]RELaw: International Workshop Series on Requirements Engineering and Law, http://gaius.isri.cmu.edu/relaw/.

[22]See the compatible functions between Eunomos and Legal-Urn in Boella et al. (2014). Both legal management systems encompass the discussions between different kind of stakeholders (lawyers, auditors, and business administrators).

5.2.2 Responsive, Smart, and Better Regulations

The Communication from the Commission of 23 March 2017 defined the strategy for governance and interoperability across the state members.[23] The EU has adopted a relational view to foster citizen participation, transparency, public monitoring and control, considering interoperability as a prerequisite "for enabling electronic communication and exchange of information between public administrations" and "for achieving a digital single market." (EU 2017). In this regard, the EU provides a set of principles and recommendations[24] to promote electronic communication across administrations, distinguishing four layers of interoperability: (i) *legal* (ensuring that organisations operating under different legal frameworks, policies and strategies are able to work together, setting interoperability checks to identify legal barriers); (ii) *organisational* (relationships between service providers and service consumers); (iii) *semantic* (developing vocabularies and schemata to describe data exchanges in the same format); (iv) *technical* (applications and infrastructures linking systems and services). More precisely:

> (i) legal issues, e.g. by ensuring that legislation does not impose unjustified barriers to the reuse of data in different policy areas; organisational aspects, e.g. by requesting formal agreements on the conditions applicable to cross-organisational interactions; data/semantic concerns, e.g. by ensuring the use of common descriptions of exchanged data; (iv) technical challenges, e.g. by setting up the necessary information systems environment to allow an uninterrupted flow of bits and bytes. [COM (2017) 134]

The European Interoperability Framework (EIF) conceptual model embraces a holistic perspective on interoperability and compliance, acknowledging the complexity of data governance.[25] This is a step towards what many years ago Nonet and Selznick (1978) called *responsive law*: "a wider sharing of legal authority", "participatory decision as a source of knowledge, a vehicle of communication, and a foundation for consent".

We will highlight three different empirical approaches—*responsive*, *smart*, and *better* regulations—which are not identical, but are devoted to the objective of getting law closer to civil society. After work done by socio-legal scholars such as Selznick, Nonet and Kazan, and activists like Ralph Nader,[26] the "responsive law"

---

[23]Brussels, 23.3.2017 COM (2017) 134 final. Source: https://eur-lex.europa.eu/resource.html?uri=cellar:2c2f2554-0faf-11e7-8a35-01aa75ed71a1.0017.02/DOC_1&format=PDF.

[24]Underlying principles for public administration are citizen- and user-centred: (i) subsidiarity and proportionality, (ii) openness, (iii) transparency, (iv) reusability, (v) technological neutrality and data portability, (vi) user-centricity, (vii) inclusion and accessibility, (viii) security and privacy, (ix) multilingualism, (x) administrative simplification, (xi) preservation of information, (xii) assessment of effectiveness and efficiency.

[25]*European Interoperability Framework—Implementation Strategy:* https://ec.europa.eu/isa2/sites/isa/files/eif_brochure_final.pdf.

[26]http://csrl.org/about/.

idea came into age and was fleshed out by legal sociologists and criminologists. How regulations and law should be approached if their main aim was empowering people? According to Braithwaite:

> Responsive regulation involves listening to multiple stakeholders and making a deliberative and flexible (responsive) choice from regulatory strategies that can be conceptually arranged in a pyramid. At the bottom of the pyramid are more frequently used strategies of first choice that are less coercive, less interventionist, and cheaper. [27]

Ayres and Braithwaite (1995) showed that compliance, respect, and cooperation in implementing regulations were possible if citizens and professional people could embrace and apply them into their everyday life. So, they should be co-involved in lawmaking, deployment and even enforcement of legislation throughout the legal drafting, implementation and eventual reform process. Between state regulation and self-regulation there are many stances that are worth exploring:

> Good policy analysis is not about choosing between the free market and government regulation. Nor is it simply deciding what the law should proscribe. If we accept that sound policy analysis is about understanding private regulation—by industry associations, by firms, by peers, and by individual consciences—and how it is interdependent with state regulation, then interesting possibilities open up to steer the mix of private and public regulation. It is this mix, this interplay, that works to assist or impede solution of the policy problem. (Ayres and Braithwaite 1995, 3).

Thus, democracy is enhanced and citizens are empowered by: (i) making choices to vote in the marketplace; (ii) voting rights in a representative democracy; (iii) participating "in any local area of collective decision making that has an important effect on their lives—in their workplace, school, local planning authority, nursing home, etc."; and (iv) standing for office, voting, and collectively participating in special-interest and public-interest associations (Ayres and Braithwaite 1995, 17).

Elaborating on top of Braithwaite's work, a related view is contended by the concept of "smart regulation", coined by Gunningham et al. (1998) for the environmental field:

> The term refers to a form of regulatory pluralism that embraces flexible, imaginative and innovative forms of social control. In doing so, it harnesses governments as well as business and third parties. For example, it encompasses self-regulation and co-regulation, using commercial interests and non-governmental organisations (NGOs) (such as peak bodies) as regulatory surrogates, together with improving the effectiveness and efficiency of more conventional forms of direct government regulation. (Gunningham and Sinclair 2017, 133)

The authors try to avoid dichotomies (government/citizens, state/market…) to focus on the plurality of regulatory forms, influences, and interactions among international standards organisations, trading partners and the supply chain, commercial institutions and financial markets, peer pressure and self-regulation through industry associations, internal environment management systems, and culture (i.e.

[27] http://johnbraithwaite.com/responsive-regulation/. See also Braithwaite (2017).

"civil society in myriad different forms") (ibid.). This leads to different design regulatory principles: (i) preferring complementary instrument mixes over single instrument approaches, (ii) less interventionist measures, (iii) escalating responses up an instrument pyramid to build in regulatory responsiveness, (iv) empowering third parties to act as surrogate regulators, (v) encouraging business to go "beyond compliance" within existing legal requirements (ibid.). Governments should bind themselves to *entice or induce* rather than enforce compliance.[28]

Both responsive and smart approaches have eventually been considered by the European Commission when launching a *better regulation* planning throughout the whole European policy cycle. Table 5.3 summarises the principles:

These principles are applied through several mandatory instruments before an initiative is launched and funds are allocated: roadmaps, Impact Assessments, fitness checks, and eventually final audits. According to the Better Regulation agenda, the EU Commission should ensure that (i) decision-making is open and transparent, (ii) citizens and stakeholders can contribute throughout the policy and law-making process, (iii) EU actions are based on evidence and understanding of the impacts, (iv) and regulatory burdens on businesses, citizens or public administrations are kept to a minimum.[29] Thus, responsive regulation is a way to cope with the "legitimacy market failure" as pointed out by Purnhagen (2015, 51): "top-down macro-economic regulation without a social bottom-up backup by the peoples of Europe has mostly failed".

Yet, it comes with limitations. This is an administrative governance model. It aims at building a EU public space that guarantees and protects citizens' rights, but it is mainly addressed to rulers, state officials and members of public administrations. While the model encompasses individual citizens, organisations, and social groups, it does not consider putting the whole framework into their hands or lending them tools to build their own regulatory systems. In this sense, it is perhaps better to take it as it is, a useful framework, or better, a component of the European governance framework linking the macro and micro-levels of public administration.

For instance, it fosters e-participation, in EU law-making processes (Schmitz et al. 2016, 2017). However, as already shown at the level of legal interoperability, *what is missing is the meso-level*. If we define linked democracy as a distributed, technologically-supported collective decision-making process, what is yet to be built is the middle-ground connectivity emerging from community-building citizenry.

It is worth mentioning in this point the impulse of legal mixed public/private business models in the new Web of Data scenarios. We are thinking of the more

[28]Thus, "the preferred role for government under smart regulation is to create the necessary preconditions for second or third parties to assume a greater share of the regulatory burden rather than engaging in direct intervention (Gunningham and Sinclair 2017, 139).

[29]https://ec.europa.eu/info/law/law-making-process/planning-and-proposing-law/better-regulation-why-and-how_en.

Table 5.3 Principles of better regulation

Embedded in the planning and policy cycle	Be well-planned and timely. All the preparatory and analytical work, including stakeholder consultations, must be done in time to feed into the policy development process
Of high quality	Be of the highest quality. The basis of any stakeholder consultation should be clear, concise and include all necessary information to facilitate responses
Evidence-based	Be based on the best available evidence including scientific advice, or a transparent explanation of why some evidence is not available and why it is still considered appropriate to act
Participatory/Open to stakeholders' views	Ensure wide participation throughout the policy cycle. Open web-based public consultations should be mandatory elements of any consultation strategy associated with and evaluation or impact assessment
Respect for subsidiarity and proportionality	EU action must be relevant and necessary, offer value beyond what Member State action alone can deliver and not go further than is necessary to resolve the problem or meet the policy objective
Comprehensive	They must consider relevant economic, social, and environmental impacts of alternative policy solutions. Stakeholders' views must be collected on all key issues
Coherent/Conducted collectively	Be coherent. New initiatives, impact assessments, consultations and evaluations must be prepared collectively by all relevant services in the framework of interservice groups
Proportionate	Be proportionate to the type of intervention or initiative, the importance of the problem or objective, and the magnitude of the expected or observed impacts
Transparent	Be clearly visible. Results of evaluations, impact assessments and consultations should be widely disseminated. Stakeholder responses should be acknowledged, and consultation results widely disseminated through a single access point. The reasons for disagreeing with dissenting views must be explained
Unbiased	Be objective and balanced. They should inform political choices with evidence—not the other way around
Appropriately resourced and organised	Be underpinned by sufficient human and financial resources to enable each evaluation, impact assessment or consultation to deliver a timely high-quality result

Source European Commission, Better Regulation Toolbox 1, Principles, Procedures & Exceptions. https://ec.europa.eu/info/sites/info/files/file_import/better-regulation-toolbox-1_en_0.pdf, 6–7

than fifty institutes of the World Legal Information Institute,[30] who have been provided with access to all kinds of legal documents since 1992 with the explicit aim of fostering the rule of law. Actually, they have been turning top-down and exclusively market-based approaches into more relational and flexible ways of

[30]See http://www.worldlii.org/, especially http://www.austlii.edu.au/ and https://www.law.cornell.edu/.

handling regulations, services, and rights. These mixed, hybrid models will probably grow and thrive in the web of data, as they encompass a flexible way to place themselves between the market, the state, and civil society. The Declaration of Free Access to Law Movement (FALM) commits them to "provide free and anonymous public access to that information" and "do not impede others from obtaining public legal information from its sources and publishing". They recently added as an objective the "development of open technical standards".[31] It is an example of an independent "connectome". The Institutes foster innovation and experimentation.[32]

5.3 Governing Linked Democracy: A Socio-Cognitive Approach

5.3.1 A Regulatory Quadrant for the Rule of Law

The field of Normative Multi-Agent Systems (NorMAS) was incepted to integrate and cope with the different notions of norms stemming from social, cognitive and computer sciences. It can be defined "as the intersection of normative systems and multiagent systems (MAS)" (Boella et al. 2007).[33]MAS are computer systems composed of multiple interacting intelligent agents, creating contexts for autonomous artificial agents.[34] Artificial Socio-cognitive systems (ASCS) contemplate this interface from a tripartite model where the affordances of the system emerge from the intersection between three dimensions—institutional, the technological and the "real world" (or social space).[35] Thus, reflecting human cogency and agency in context—its 'cognitive ecology'. We will start from this same point to define legal linked data systems or, *tout court*, socio-legal ecosystems.

Hutchins defined *cognitive ecology* as "the study of cognitive phenomena in context" (Hutchins 2010, 705–6). The term points to "the web of mutual dependence among the elements of a cognitive ecosystem":

> Everything is connected to everything else. Fortunately, not all connectivity is equally dense. […]. To speak of cognitive ecology is to employ an obvious metaphor, that cognitive systems are in some specific way like biological systems. In particular, it points to the web of mutual dependence among the elements of an ecosystem. (Hutchins 2010, ibid.)

---

[31]http://www.falm.info/declaration/.

[32]Greenleaf (2009), Casellas et al. (2012), Greenleaf et al. (2013), Vallbé and Casellas (2014), Curtotti et al. (2015).

[33]See Andrighetto et al. (2013) for a general view; for norMAS and law, Casanovas et al. (2014a).

[34]On MAS applications see Sierra (2004), Christiaanse and Hulstijn (2012), and especially the survey carried out by Müller and Fischer (2014).

[35]See Noriega et al. (2014), Christiaanse et al. (2014), Christiaanse and Hulstijn (2012). In 2016, their *Manifesto for conscious design* introduces the notion of Hybrid Online Social Systems (HOSS) and situates them at the centre of the triangle: the impact of AI affects everyday life (Noriega et al. 2016). On the notion of 'coordination' for norMAS, see Aldewereld et al. (2016).

Hutchins draws on Bateson's metaphor of the "blind man" to further illustrate his point. To explain the locomotion of a blind man with a stick, "you will need the street, the stick, the man, the street, the stick, and so on, round and round" (ibid.). The metaphor also echoes Herbert Simon's ant's path, and the second order isomorphism fallacy.[36]

Creating a socio-legal ecosystem requires an appraisal of the dynamic coupling between the social environment, the actors and the tools and technologies they use to reach their objectives and recreate their social bonds. It involves experimentation, plasticity and sensitivity. The outcomes of this interplay can also be conceived as *thinking without representation*. For example, collective action *emerges* from a set of conditions and coordinated actions that constitute the system, allowing multiple possibilities to deploy in one direction or another. This *enaction*[37] perspective does not exclude the role of collective emotions in the making of regulatory schemes, as the cognitive properties of groups are different from the cognitive properties of any individual in the group.

The idea of complex *intermediation* is crucial to create sustainable socio-legal ecosystems on the web. Again, in the first edition of *The Sciences of the Artificial* (1969), Simon introduced the property of *near-decomposability* of systems: sub-systems can have stronger links within them than between them. The second edition (1984), which includes a new chapter on the social world, shows how coordination in a complex system is complex at every level of the system. We could benefit from these ideas, as the components of a regulatory system also exhibit the plasticity and diversity of near-decomposable systems.

When it comes to the social implementation of the rule of law—either through Artificial Socio-cognitive Technical Systems (ASCS), Hybrid Online Social Systems (HOSS), or Open Linked Data (OLD) systems—it is possible to identify basic components and the relations between them looking at the sources, domains, and position with respect to citizens (bindingness of norms or rules). Rather than discrete categories or lists of requirements, it is a matter of degree and conditions of values and principles. In a way, this is previous to building any kind of ontology or artificial tool. We are dealing with the pragmatic dimension of the rule of law, i.e. its *governance*.

To start with, we could figure out the implementation of the rule of law along two different relational dimensions at the empirical level: (i) material institutional power [force, *macht*, *fuerza, forza*], (ii) and social dialogue (negotiation,

[36]First-order isomorphism describes the situation in which a similarity relation exists between an internal representation and the real-world object being represented (Shepard and Chipman 1970). Second-order isomorphism refers to a similarity relation that exists between the similarities among internal representations and the corresponding similarities among multiple real-world objects being represented (Shepard and Chipman 1970). As famously depicted in *The Sciences of the Artificial* (1969), an ant, viewed as a behaving system, is quite simple. The apparent complexity of its behaviour over time is largely a reflection of the complexity of the environment in which it finds itself. Complexity is in the environment, not in the ant.

[37]'Enaction' is the notion that organisms create their own experience through their actions in a dynamic and multi-modal way. We are assuming that this holds as well for social groups or communities.

compromise, mediation, agreement). Thinking of law and regulations, power and how it is handled and eventually shared, matters. Even at the micro-level, the alignment of Linked Democracy properties with Ostrom's Common Pool Resources principles (Fig. 4.3) maintains a proportioned and gradual system of sanctions. There is a wide range of sanctions, from incentives to criminal punishment. But we are looking for some value to be assigned to them according to the degree of 'bindingness' of norms and the acceptance of stakeholders.

The intuition to first separate binding from non-binding norms according to the nature of the objectives and procedures is implicitly assumed by many formulations. For instance, Brous et al. (2016) produced a long list of principles for data governance in their systematic review. They eventually distilled four principles of data governance for public organizations—organisation, alignment [with the needs of the business], compliance [monitoring and enforcement], and common understanding [of data quality]. But, "data quality is often related to 'fitness for use' and data governance demands binding guidelines and rules for data quality management". Likewise, when searching for requirements for an architecture framework for pan-European E-Government services, Mondorf and Wimmer (2016) used a nuanced concept of compliance (and the bindingness of agreements). They applied the notion of "enterprise architecture", a concept used to deal with organisational complexity and interoperability. The EU Better Regulations scheme for interoperability has also been structured within this framework. The Open Group Architecture Framework (TOGAF) is developing the technical architecture to make it applicable: the EIRA legal view equally splits up legal regulations into binding and non-binding instruments.[38]

Figure 5.2 below plots our regulatory quadrant for the rule of law. The validity of norms (i.e. their 'legality') emerges from four different types of regulatory frames, with some distinctive properties. Properties are understood here as correlating dynamic patterns. But this is only a preliminary scheme, a conceptual compass to be used for a first clustering of norms, according to their type and degree of compliance: *abidance* (for hard law), *conformance* (for policies), *accordance* (for soft law), and *congruence* (or congruity) for ethics. According to the degree of abstraction at the implementation level, these four categories can be blurred into overlapping concepts. Agreements can be understood as mandatories; in practice, corporate policies can be more binding than some statutes. Actually, the concept of "negative compliance" or "noncompliance" is used to denote corporate strategies to avoid legal abidance when compliance is deemed to be too expensive or contrary to the business interests (Mun 2015).

[38]"A [Public Policy] is the outcome of a specific [Public Policy Cycle] that aims at addressing the needs of a group of stakeholders. The policy is formulated and implemented with the help of [Public Policy Formulation and Implementation Instruments] such as [Legal Requirements or Constraints] in the form of either [Binding Instruments] or [Non-Binding Instruments], or [Operational Enablers], such as [Financial Resources] or [Implementing Guidelines]." See "Legal view" TOGAF (2017, 39).

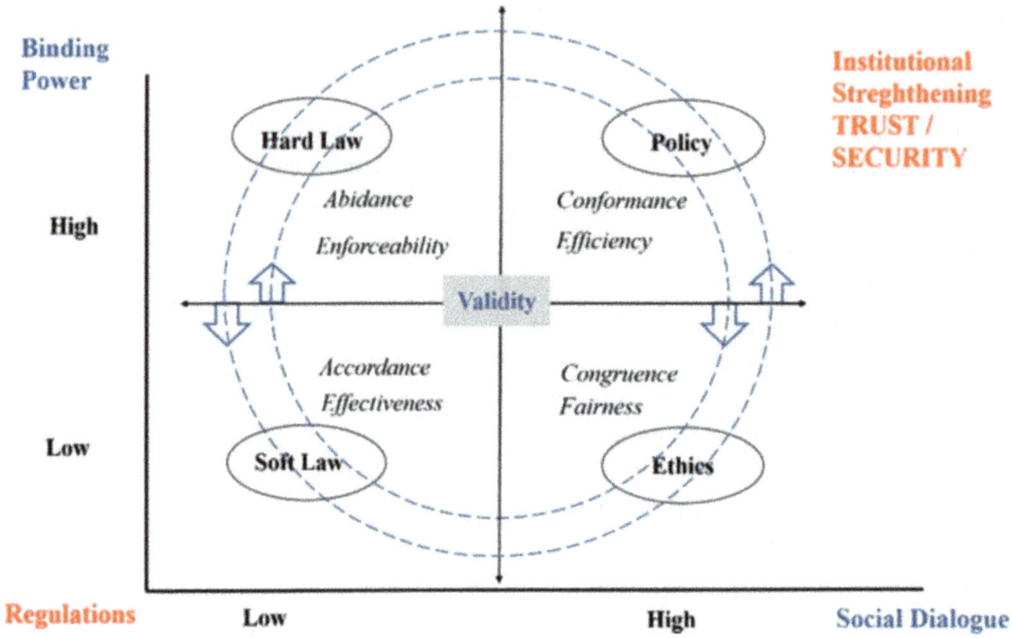

Fig. 5.2 Regulatory quadrant for the rule of law

5.3.2 *Types of Legal Governance*

Hard law refers to legally binding obligations, either in the national or international arena, under regulations that can lead to adjudication court processes. *Soft law*, on the contrary, is usually not mandatory. It consists of non-legally binding rules, best practices, and principles that facilitate the governance of networks, social organizations, companies, and institutions. Soft law makes room for dialogue, negotiations, and shared decisions by relevant actors and interested stakeholders. In the quadrant, soft and hard law are non-discrete categories situated on a *continuum* that allows the coordination of different powers and authorities to produce *global law* and regulations across borders involving citizens, organizations, and states (Karlsson-Vinkhuyzen and Vihma 2009).

> International actors choose softer forms of legalized governance when those forms offer superior institutional solutions. […]. The realm of soft law begins once legally arrangements are weakened along one or more of the dimensions of obligation, precision, and delegation. This softening can occur in varying degrees along each dimension and in different combinations across dimensions. We use the shorthand term *soft law* to distinguish this broad class of deviations from hard law – and, at the other extreme, from purely political arrangements in which legalization is largely absent. But bear in mind that soft law comes in many varieties: the choice between hard law and soft law is not a binary one (Abbot and Snidal 2000, 421–422).

As recently evaluated by D'Rosario and Zeleznikow (2018), we should not underestimate the force of soft law, as it evidences the role of market forces and bilateral and multi-lateral pressures on legal implementation. d'Aspremont et al. (2017) have also highlighted this point as a social source of International Law.

Policy is usually defined as a "a set of ideas, or a plan of what to do in particular situations, that has been agreed officially by a group of people, a business organization, a government, or a political party."[39] It refers to *policies* designed, enacted, and implemented by corporations, companies, nation-states or international agencies and organisations. Policies cannot be understood as soft law when they are enacted by government agencies that have the capacity of enforcing them by means of sanctions, fines and lawsuits. There is a phenomenon of osmosis or hybridization between government administrations and agencies, and corporate governance. Government agencies tend to be drawn on corporate organisational and, especially, information and data-driven models. However, public governance is and should be kept separate from the private one (including companies and corporations).

Corporate governance is a broad category than can also be considered as a form of policy-making. It includes methodologies, models and standards developed over the last twenty-five years (for example, ISO standards related to corporate and regulatory compliance and security). Some models for IT Governance are drawn from COSO, COBIT, ISO 27002 (ISO 17799) and ISO 38500.[40] There are also best practices and standards set by international professional organisations. ISO/IEC 27001[41] is an information security standard published by the International Organization for Standardization (ISO) and by the International Electrotechnical Commission (IEC), entitled *Information technology—Security techniques—Code of practice for information security management*.[42] Standards for the representation of vocabularies on the Semantic Web have been recently considered by ISOs on thesaurus. The new ISO 25964 is close to the SKOS approach and includes a data model. It is divided into two parts: (i) Thesauri for information retrieval, (ii) Interoperability with other vocabularies.[43]

W3C recommendations and standards on linked open data also fall within this category (policy/governance). Developers adopting them benefit from their wide acceptance. Yet, standards are not expected to gain compliance but *conformance*. They refer to the quality of coding and markup tools such as Hypertext Markup

---

[39]https://dictionary.cambridge.org/dictionary/english/policy.

[40]This standard is based on the AS 8015-2005 Australian Standard for Corporate Governance of Information and Communication Technology (2005).

[41]http://www.iso27001security.com/html/27002.html.

[42]See also (i) ISO 17799 (developed today by ISO 27001/02), a guide for implementing a set of policies, practices and procedures to consolidate the information security administered by an organization, (ii) ISO/IEC 27002, which requires that management systematically examines the organization's information security risks, taking account of the threats, vulnerabilities and impacts; (iii) Clause 6.1.3 of ISO/27001:2013, describes how an organisation can respond to risks with a risk treatment plan; an important part of this is choosing appropriate controls; (iv) ISO/IEC 27002 seeking the preservation of confidentiality, integrity, and availability.

[43]*ISO 25964: Information and documentation—Thesauri and interoperability with other vocabularies.* See the presentation by the project lead (Clarke and Stella 2011).

Language (HTML) and Cascading Style Sheets (CSS) and allow validators to check the conformance of web coding to them.[44]

Both ISO/IECs and W3C standards can be conceived as forms of soft law, network or multi-stake holder governance. Yet, these latter concepts have a broader regulatory scope, intended to solve political and social disputes in regional, national, and international arenas (e.g. *conflicts* between social groups, corporations, companies, sub-state and state entities).

We can consider different types of governance that would fall under the policy label—mainly *internet, network,*[45] *stakeholder,*[46] *data, and algorithmic governance.*[47] Cap 1 has briefly presented some of them. Data and algorithmic governance are especially relevant to expand the protections of the rule of law.

We should differentiate Internet governance from the forms of contemporary governance on the web. The latter has been increasingly introduced through the combination of algorithms, semantic languages, computational linguistics, data mining,[48] visualization, and, recently, Artificial Intelligence methods (such as deep machine learning).[49] They are ambiguously referred to as "big data".[50] Some prudence is required here: after their extended review, Sivarajah et al. (2017, 279) conclude that strengthening empirical research based on in-depth case studies, and qualitative and quantitative research, is much needed as "most of the articles analysed followed an analytical approach".

A functional typology of algorithmic selection applications is offered by Just and Latzer (2017): (i) search, (ii) aggregation, (iii) surveillance, (iv) forecast, (v) filtering, (vi) recommendation, (vii) scoring, (viii) content production, (ix) and allocation. Each one of them constitute separate domains of computer expertise, understood as a governance "institutional steering", a "horizontal and vertical extension of traditional government", looking *beyond* public and private actors (e.g. governments and industry) and, vertically, looking beyond multi-stakeholder instruments. Social reality is now increasingly shaped and constructed by algorithmic selection (ibid.).

---

[44]http://validator.w3.org/, http://jigsaw.w3.org/css-validator/.

[45]Rhodes (2007), Provan and Kenis (2008), Gottschalk (2009).

[46]On the notion of 'stake-holder governance', Hens and Bhaskar (2005); on its structure and processes applied to the Internet, Malcolm (2008, 2015); on "stake-holder democracy", MacDonald (2008), MacDonald and MacDonald (2017); for a critical view see Bäckstrand (2006), Fransen and Kolk (2007), Bexell et al. (2010).

[47]Cfr. The surveys by Chen and Zhang (2014), Siddiqa et al. (2016); cfr. also, on algorithmic governance, the typology by Just and Latzer (2017).

[48]I.e. Correlation and regression analysis; and data classification, clustering, prediction, and diagnosis (Zhao-Hong et al. 2018, 205)

[49]See the surveys on data-intensive applications (Chen and Zhang 2014), big data life-cycles and management (Khan et al. 2014) big data management (Siddiqa et al. 2016), big data analytics in governance (Bhardwaj and Singh 2017), on data processing methods (Zhao-Hong et al. 2018).

[50]It is commonly described as data satisficing a 5-V model: (i) Volume (data scale datasets), (ii) Value (low density, high value information), (iii) Variety (including unstructured and semi-structured data), (iv) Velocity (speed of data collection and analysis), (v) Validity (quality and veracity of data).

Thus, the problem is now how to assemble, monitor, use and control these different methods. Semantic matching to identify related information, re-engineering, re-using, model-driven engineering and graph analysis operating on an ontological basis are some of the techniques that the semantic web community is developing. *Smart data* is related to the 5-V model (see note 113): "an organized way to semantically compile, manipulate, correlate, and analyse different data sources" (Duong et al. 2017) that is adding value to governance and decision-making. From a regulatory point of view, there are several challenges related to them: security and data protection, ownership, privacy, data flows exchange and cross-border data flows. After the enactment of the European GDPR this is a hot topic, with countless contributions.

We would like to point out just one challenge that is key to the linked democracy approach. In Table 5.1 we aligned Ostrom's CPR principles—rules in use matched to local needs and conditions, participation, self-monitoring, need of proportional sanctions…—with the substantive principles of the rule of law. This is a new version of the so-called micro-macro link problem. Ostrom's principles are community-driven. How could polycentric governance be compatible with data-driven societies? Pitt et al. (2013, 40) contend that

> Collective awareness can be achieved by analysing big data generated by networked sensors and devices as well as ICT-enabled users. Search, data mining, and visualization technologies make it possible to spot trends and predict the trajectories of higher-level variables. This in turn enables collective action, without which it might be impossible to change community behaviour to reach a desirable outcome—for example, sustaining a scarce resource.

Social intelligence, collective action modelling entails a shift both in governance and legal studies. Our contention is that collective awareness can also be carried out within the framework of the meta-rule of law.

Finally, *Ethics* primarily refer to morals, social mores, practical knowledge and principles that should be implemented into legal regulations, policies, and governance structures. But, most interestingly, ethics can be infused across them.[51]

Ethics and law were not mentioned in the first accounts on the semantic web (e.g. Bizer et al. 2011), but this is experiencing a dramatic turn. The defence of ethical values embedded into computer systems, Multi-Agent Systems (MAS) and Artificial Intelligence is a hot topic now, bringing together (i) *thoroughness* (the sound implementation of what the system is intended to do), (ii) *mindfulness* (those aspects that affect the individual users, and stakeholders) and (iii) *responsibility* (the values that affect others) (Noriega et al. 2016).

---

[51]We can identify schematically at least four stages in privacy and data protection related to ethical principles. This is a well-known history: (i) the inception of *Fair Information Practice Principles* (FIPs) that were published in 1973 by the Advisory Committee on Automated Personal Data Systems in the Department of Health, Education and Welfare (USA) under the inspiration of Alan Westin; (ii) the proposal of a *unifying identity metasystem layer* by the Microsoft Chief Architect Kim Cameron in his blog in 2005; (iii) the proposal of Privacy-by-design principles (PbD) issued by Ann Cavoukian in 2006; (iv) the development of PbD and by default in the General Data Protection Reform launched by the EU in 2012 that led to the new EU Regulation that came into force in May 2018.

The *Onlife Manifesto* (Floridi 2015) reflects on the fading distinction between reality, virtuality, human, machine, and nature that seems to be prevalent in our hyperconnected world. The authors elaborate on the notion of complexity (see Pagallo 2015; Pagallo et al. 2018) and MAS to question (or nuance) the role of the nation-state in web of data environments.

Dignum (2018) has shown that ethics and AI are related at several levels: (i) *Ethics-by-Design* (EbD, "the technical/algorithmic integration of ethical reasoning capabilities as part of the behaviour of artificial autonomous system"), (ii) *Ethics-in-Design* (EiD, "the regulatory and engineering methods that support the analysis and evaluation of the ethical implications of AI systems as these integrate or replace traditional social structures"), (iii) and *Ethics-for-Design* (EfD, "the codes of conduct, standards and certification processes that ensure the integrity of developers and users as they research, design, construct, employ and manage artificial intelligent systems").

We also deem all three levels necessary to implement the principles of the rule of law beyond the boundaries of the nation state and to develop socio-legal ecosystems.

5.4 Governing Linked Democracy: Socio-Legal Ecosystems

5.4.1 Socio-Legal Ecosystems

The term 'ecosystem', coined by Arthur Tansley in 1935, originated in biology and ecology studies. In ecology, the term points to the coexistence of living and non-living organisms in a niche, or "integration of *all* biological *(biotic)* and nonbiological *(abiotic)* parts" and "monitoring the *movement of energy* and *materials* (water, chemicals, nutrients, pollutants, etc.) into and out of its boundaries" (Vogt et al. 1997, 71). The concept was later adopted, among many other disciplines, by cybernetics, meaning the interface and exchange of information in complex systems within their environments (i.e. within social and natural contexts). Gregory Bateson entitled the collection of his works *Towards an Ecology of Mind* (1972). This is the tradition we choose to situate our own use of the term, familiar to cognitive sciences and cognitive ecology, along with 'situated meaning' and 'situated cognition'.

The notion of 'legal ecosystem' has also been recently used in professional studies, referring to the involvement of all legal professionals and stakeholders (Brenton 2017). In computer sciences and law, it has been employed to wrap up the methodology that involves the participation of end-users in the knowledge acquisition process (Governatori et al. 2009). We will use the notion of 'legal linked data ecosystm' or, *tout court*, 'socio-legal ecosystem' in a different way, *meaning all processes, interactions and exchange of information involved in the social and cultural implementation of a regulatory system, including its design, monitoring, and users' compliance and behaviour*. We will point out the dynamic properties of its normative elements and its institutional settings.

If we assume the essential socio-cognitive framework described above, it appears that we cannot generate a legal ecosystem by just laying down, enacting, or publishing a law or regulation in an official site. In most cases of public law, this can be considered a necessary non-sufficient condition. Nevertheless, the system should also be understood, accepted, and settled under the social conditions that guarantee its implementation. We contend that legal ecosystems are not just generated from the enactment of laws: they emerge from a set of conditions amongst human and technical interactions, including the requirements of artificial systems and the individual and collective behaviour of their users.

Zuiderwijk et al. (2014) have suggested a number of actions and four key elements when building Open Data (OD) ecosystems: (i) releasing and publishing open data on the internet, (ii) searching, finding, evaluating and viewing data and their related licenses, (iii) cleansing, analysing, enriching, combining, linking and visualizing data, and (iv) interpreting and discussing data and providing feedback to the data provider and other stakeholders. To integrate the full set of required elements they add three additional elements: (v) user pathways showing directions for how open data can be used, (vi) a quality management system and (vii) different types of metadata to be able to connect the elements. Thus, an OD ecosystem consists of a multilayered and plural framework: (i) "an open data ecosystem is characterized by multiple interdependent socio-technical levels, dimensions, actors (including data providers, infomediaries and users), elements and components", and (ii) "need to address challenges related to policy, licenses, technology, financing, organization, culture, and legal frameworks and are influenced by ICT infrastructures" (Zuiderwijk et al. 2014, 29–30).

However, to turn these kind of OD ecosystems into legal ones, we should delineate more precisely how all these elements can be related to the whole regulatory system (not only to the type of license at stake) and to agency. Hence, we would need to articulate a scheme (or meta-model) that could be used (i) to flesh out the three dimensions plotted in Fig. 10 (legal, social and semantic), (ii) to differentiate the properties of the regulatory system and the meta-rule scheme for the rule of law, (iii) to embed privacy/data/security and compliance by-design into computer systems, (iv) to situate and implement them into specific environments, (iv) and to embed the protections of the rule of law into the meta-rule of law through formal representations of norms and rights. All components, functions and activities that the construction of an OD ecosystem entails should be evaluable and evaluated.

Moreover, social ecosystems are complex, and micro-agent interaction and change can lead to a macro-system evolution (Mitleton-Kelly and Papaefthimiou 2002). Some feed-back processes are associated with them. In the case of the rule of law, both positive and negative feedback are present: the goal of producing trust and security through institutional strengthening mechanisms tends to create stability, which is one of the features to make a socio-legal ecosystem sustainable; but the whole process is not teleologically-driven, i.e. some changes in the system are not intended. Socio-legal systems are cultural, in a broad sense. Thus, "a plethora of interacting and interconnected micro-feedback-processes whose connectivity and interaction creates emergent macro-feedback-processes and structures" (Mitleton-Kelly and Papaefthimiou 2002, 272). Excessive control mechanisms and inflexible rule-driven organisations can be counterproductive.

Figures 5.3, 5.4 and 5.5 are complementary. The first one is Braithwaite-like, similar to the pyramids for regulatory theory (responsive and smart regulations) drawn by Braithwaite, Gunningham, Grabosky and Sinclair, among others (Drahos 2017). We used an almost identical one to plot the levels of "formality" in mediation: from *implicit* to *explicit* dialogue, and from *non-binding law* to *binding law* (Casanovas et al. 2011, Intr.). Processes and outcomes could be accommodated into it, from natural mediation to legal mediation. Interestingly enough, this could illuminate the artificial model to support mediation that Noriega et al. (2011) articulated as an electronic institution, as the problem that emerged out of it was *the legal value of the agreement*. When can an artificially-driven procedure 'count as' legal? When can procedural moves through different steps be considered as 'legal'?

Artefacts and e-institutions are tools, and as such can be used informally as well. Only when the e-institution is nested into a social set of relationships that assert the degree and value of its "affordances"—the effectiveness and efficiency of its internal moves and steps in a given environment—the outcome can hold not only as formally or 'normatively' valid, but as 'legally' valid as well. The term 'affordance' is an interesting concept. It denotes the properties of the environment that are perceived, endorsed and eventually modified by the agents' actions. From this perspective, the 'validity' ('legality') of a right, norm, or a set of norms can be understood as a complex outcome of the affordances of the system.

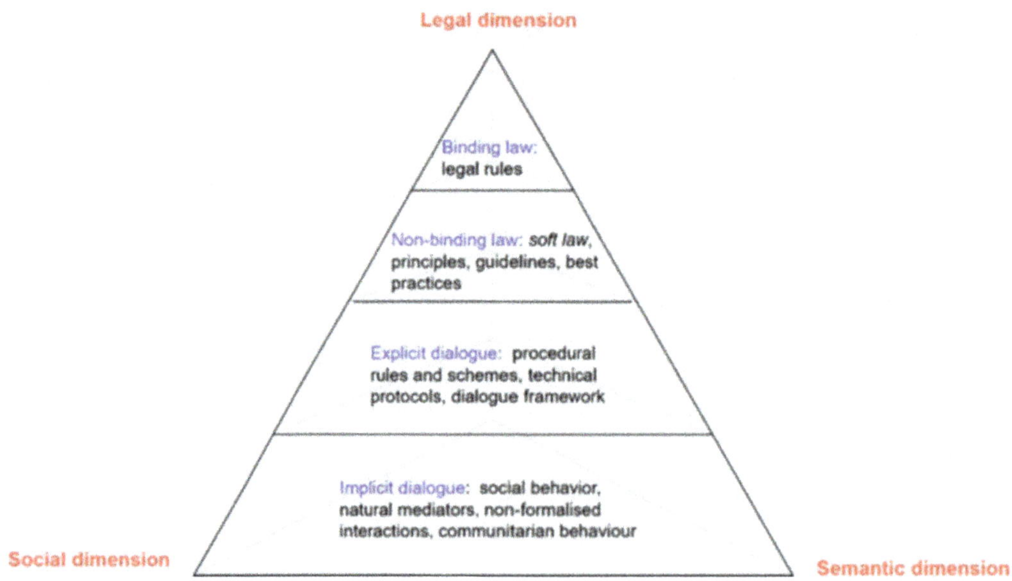

Fig. 5.3 From social informal dialogue to legal formal power

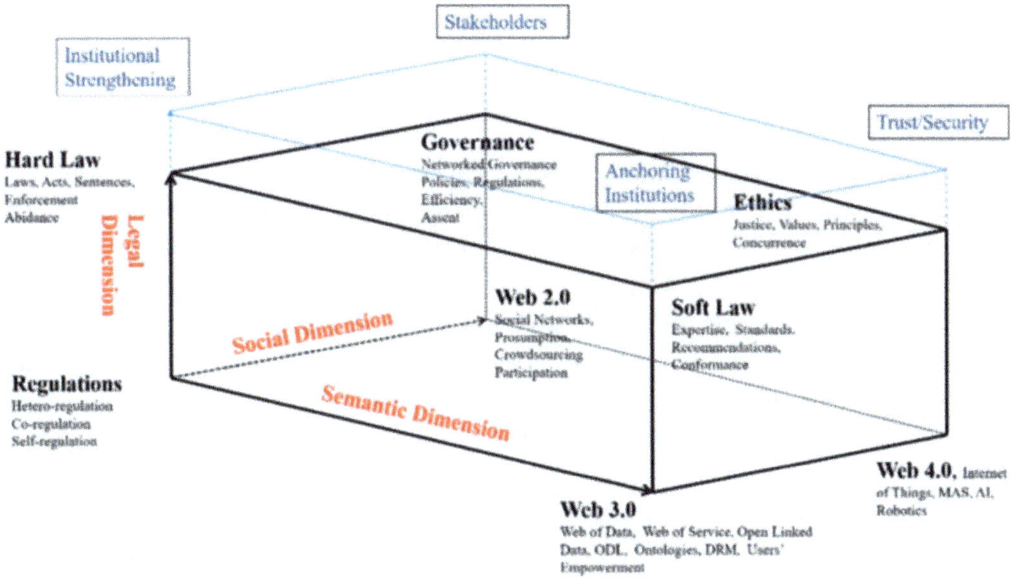

Fig. 5.4 Socio-legal ecosystems pragmatic layer

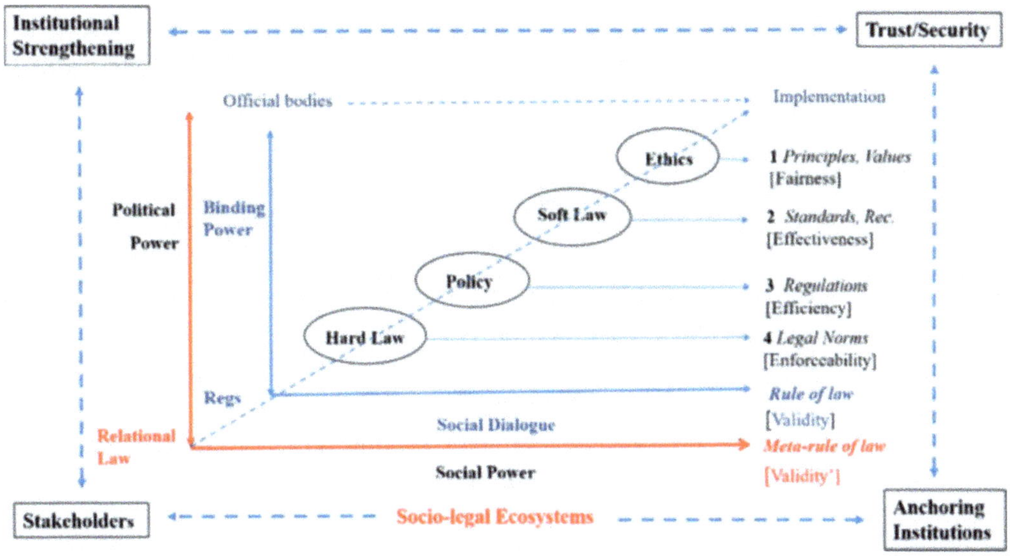

Fig. 5.5 Meta-model for socio-legal ecosystems (Meta-rule of law)

5.4.2 *A Meta-Model for the Implementation of the Rule of Law*

Thus, the problem for validity is not just that the collective processes coming from the grassroots, bottom-up, should be "legally" compliant with norms to also acquire a legal value, but that legality itself might show different values and degrees of accomplishment.

'Validity' [*Geltung, validez, validità, validité*] is defined in analytical theory as the property which captures for any rule or norm the quality of belonging to a legal system. Usually, a 'valid' norm is deemed to be a 'legal norm'. And, to acquire this quality of law, a rule or norm is expected to be (or become) *valid*.[52] In legal theory, the definition has recently turned from a conception in which validity was considered as a feature of norms or system of norms to a discursive one, in which the law comes into being by means of the argumentation process stemming from them (legal argumentation) (Grabowski 2013). This is partially leaning on previous works on defeasible logic and argumentation by H. Prakken and G. Sartor, among others, drawing an inferential theoretical approach to legal systems in wich rules are understood as 'inferential links'.[53]

We deem our approach compatible with a normative, discursive or logical definition of validity (Araszkiewicz and Casanovas 2016). Validity in these latter senses refers to the regulatory model built by the analyst, i.e. it holds for the regulatory model that it is built as discourse, reasoning, argumentation or knowledge; but to make it 'legal', i.e. *admissible*, requires the satisfaction of another set of conditions that are depending on the contextual field of application and on the regulatory sources at hand. From this standpoint, validity depends upon other properties—i.e. affordances—running along two different axes (binding power, social dialogue), and it *emerges* as a property from the functioning of the whole system (including human and artificial agents). Regulations unfold along an institutional *continuum*. Validity is a characteristic feature of such a *continuum*, a property pertaining and emerging from the whole regulatory system which is essentially dynamic and related to the interactive behaviour of agents. From this standpoint, it does not 'supervene', but 'emerges' once first order properties—enforceability, efficiency, effectiveness, and fairness (criteria for justice)—reach a pre-determined threshold. Hence, what becomes gradually 'valid' is the whole system, as the actual presence (as a fact) of its components make it happen (in many ways). This is close to the idea of *pragmatic web* advanced by Singh (2002a) in the early days of the Semantic Web: "semantics in a manner that is reusable across applications, the priority of process over data, the importance of interaction, and the critical need for accommodating user context" (Singh 2002b).[54]

[52]We will follow up here the discussion initiated in Casanovas (2012), and followed in Casanovas (2015a, b, 2017) and Araszkiewicz and Casanovas (2016). An early example, Casanovas et al. (2006).

[53]Sartor (2009a) contends that 'intermediate legal concepts' (such as 'property') are the concepts through which legal norms convey both legal consequences and preconditions of further legal effects. In Sartor (2009b) he contends that there is a tension between their inferential and ontological meaning, and that both sides are required to make sense of legal norms.

[54]See the *Pragmatic Web Manifesto* (Schoop et al. 2006), and our position in Casanovas et al. (2017a).

Figure 5.4 represents the necessary meta-level that can be added on top of Fig. 5.1 to ground validity on the three regulatory dimensions of the Web—legal, social and linguistic. Figure 5.5 depicts the meta-model we propose to cope with this complexity.

We are facing *hybrid* environments, partly human, and partly created by artificial agents or languages (linked data). To operationalise a regulatory system, to integrate its three dimensions into a specific environment and make it 'legal', we need to figure out some more elements: (i) the institutional strengthening of some type of positive law or rights; (ii) the behaviour of stakeholders (creating, using, and participating proactively in its creation, modification and eventual substitution); (iii) the production of security and trust (as a result: they are never directly produced but reached); (iv) the presence of intermediate institutions created to "anchor" the properties of the system—i.e. its affordances—into the social space.

From an empirical point of view, 'validity' can be conceptually defined as a *second order property, a four-tuple function of ethics (fairness), policies (efficiency), soft law (effectiveness) and hard law (enforceability)*, emerging from the ecosystem. This definition facilitates the application of metrics to measure the *institutional strengthening* of the system; i.e. the coordinated organization of normative components for specific platforms, apps or other devices applying semantic technologies. We do not yet have a composite indicator for legal validity (i.e. for assigning legality)—just a preliminary attempt (Ciambra and Casanovas 2014)—but it would be useful for assessing the legal value of the strength, scope and performance of the regulatory system.

Figure 5.5 provides more perspectives on the components and the layered dynamics of the meta-model. Within this approach, several levels of 'validity' can be distinguished: (a) validity as a product of the official norms enacted by an official body (this is the classical definition); (b) as the *composite* product of official norms, multi-layered stakeholder governance, negotiations (dialogue), and ethics (values); (c) as the product of the internal process of rule-representation in some formal language (legalXML, legalRuleML)—meta-rule of law—; (d) as the social regulatory product within the socio-legal ecosystem. Let´s call them (i) *positive* validity; (ii) *composite* validity; (iii) *formal* validity; (iv) and *ecological* validity.

Ecological validity is a popular term in psychology. It refers to the extent the results of the research can be linked or referred to predict behaviour and situations in everyday life (i.e. in different contexts and scenarios). Aaron Cicourel cautions that it can only be *approximated* in the social and behavioural sciences.[55] Our use of the term refers to the extent a normative system or regulatory model is anchored and institutionalised within a specific legal ecosystem. In this sense, it relates to the way that abidance, accordance, conformance and congruence with norms are

[55]"Validity in the non-experimental social sciences refers to the extent to which complex organizational activities represented by aggregated data from public and private sources and demographic and sample surveys can be linked to the collection, integration, and assessment of temporal samples of observable (and when possible recordable) activities in daily life settings." (Cicourel 2007, 736)

effectively materialized, and the affordances that the regulatory system puts into play and offers to the (human or artificial) agents, depending on how it has been designed.

Recent research on the semantic relationships established by Hohfeld—the eight "jural" relationships included into the two classical squares of opposites and correlatives[56]—has shown that they can be remodelled using Petri nets.[57] They can be conceptualised from an interactional perspective. This leads to the idea of understanding the environment and the intentions of action (they can be negative as well) to set the position and roles of players (as the authors say, a scheme of a seem-to-be normal sale may hide a money-laundering scheme). Rights and duties are referred to this semantically enriched patterns to start modelling, i.e. to embed more complex specific situations into a formal representation language.

This is a good place to recall Ostrom's design principles for sustainable management (CPR). Pitt and Diaconescu (2015) apply the idea of complex intermediate autonomous sub-systems to develop the polycentricism of governance in self-organised institutions.[58] For example, when considering the possibility to set communities that control their own energy infrastructure, Pitt and Diaconescu (2015) note that excessive demand, which would otherwise lead to a power outage, could be pre-empted with co-dependent institutions that use social capital to stabilise their inter-operations. However, they also observe that rules alone are not enough to implement it:

> Co-dependence between socio-technical systems with shared resources implies that such systems cannot run in isolation and follow completely independent rule sets. Indeed, co-dependence requires coordination via dedicated institutions, the management of which is critical to the sustainability and endurance of the resulting system of co-dependent systems.

In this case, the ecological validity of the system depends on how well the institutional coordination of the co-dependence works. But there are many other situations in which the focal point, i.e. the salient features of the outcome that produces coordination[59], will be related to sanctions, motivation, understanding or habit of the members of the community (Gunderson and Cosens 2018). Behavioural compliance and ecological validity are closely related (Casanovas and Oboler 2018).

---

[56] I *Jural Opposites*: Right/No Right; Privilege/Duty; Power/Disability; Immunity/Liability. II *Jural Correlatives*: Right/Duty; Privilege/No-right; Power/Liability; Immunity/Disability.

[57] Sileno (2016, 161 and ff.), Sileno et al. (2014, 2015).

[58] Pitt and Diaconescu draw from Koestler's notion of 'holon' (something that is simultaneously a whole and a part): "a holonic system (or holarchy) is composed of "a *holonic system (or holarchy)* is composed of interrelated subsystems, each of which are in turn composed of sub-subsystems and so on, recursively, until reaching a lowest level of 'elementary' subsystems" (ibid.).

[59] We borrow the use of the term 'salience' and 'focal point' from McAdams and Nadler (2008).

5.4.3 Semantic Web Regulatory Models (SWRM)

The meta-model depicted in Fig. 5.5 allows the assessment of 'legality' or 'validity' to embed the protections and values of the rule of law into modelling—SW languages, NorMAS, ASCS. To regulate processing and the outcomes of an information system on a platform, e.g., several sources are usually used at different dimensions and levels of organization. Take privacy, for instance. It begins to take shape in the semantic field (Kirrane et al. 2018). There is a pool of norms coming from different organisms and settings, including statutes, case law, policies, standards, best practices… Norms are not just there: they are first selected, interpreted, constructed, combined and eventually implemented by means of a set of intermediary processes into regulatory models. Moreover, to ingrain legal rights into computer models, a process of correlating and mapping design strategies, e.g. against privacy and data protection patterns, must be put in place.

Working on the modelling strategy, Colesky and Ghanavati (2016) have proposed to add a further level of abstraction that they define as *tactic*. Strategy "specifies a distinct architectural goal in privacy by design to achieve a certain level of privacy protection", while tactics is "an approach to privacy by design which contributes to the goal of an overarching privacy design strategy". Therefore, in the line of goal-oriented requirements engineering, they flesh out the "quality attribute" for privacy strategies regarding data, i.e. (i) enforce, (ii) demonstrate, (iii) control, (iv) inform, (v) minimise, (vi) abstract, (vii) separate, (viii) and hide. This is related to semantic compliance.

There are at least three ways to embed Privacy by Design (PbD) into modelling (design planning): (i) direct strategy (*compliance by design*, as it was classically understood by Cavoukian), (ii) tactics (*near compliance*, as defined by Colesky and Ghavanati (2016) and (iii) *indirect strategy* (compliance *through* design). The notion of 'near compliance' reflects the difficulties of modelling legal rights: "software designed with compliance in mind from the beginning, resulting in less legal consultant work". The notion of 'compliance through design' tries to encompass not only legal requirements but the systemic interoperability that is needed to model affordances and socio-legal conditions.

An indirect strategy is subjected to some more requirements, as it embraces a pragmatic approach. It comprises the information flow, the organisation, the functions and affordances of the technological device, the roles of designers, controllers and end-users, including lawyers or consultants that participate all along the process, in which ontology building is one of the components to enhancing and implementing rights (Casanovas et al. 2014b). Thus, semantic interoperability is one of the objectives to be reached, but *legal compliance* is deemed to have a deeper and larger scope than *regulatory compliance*. *Compliance-by design* (CbD) and *Compliance-through design* (CtD) can be distinguished according to the structure, components, and the nature of their effects.[60]

This is especially relevant for the implementation of the meta-rule of law, because the way that rights (and especially political rights) are defined sets a normative and institutional framework in which all citizens exercise and perform their freedom and specific liberties. These liberties have a transnational and global scope and have been conceptualised in a number of political philosophies. We have recently summarised their ethical scope in four dimensions, elaborating on Walzer's, Nussbaum's, and Floridi's formulations: (i) *complex equality* (justice could be adjudicated across distinct distributive spheres, in order to respect the differences and harmonise social goods, wealth, political office, commodities, education, security, health…), (ii) *contextual integrity* (adequate selection and enactment of rights to norms of specific contexts) (iii) *ontology* (not to be confused with computer ontologies, it refers to fundamental ethical concepts), (iv) and *algorithmic governance*. By doing this, we intended to address the bases for setting the relationships between linked democracy and the meta-rule of law (Casanovas et al. 2017b).

We will stress now that to foster socio-legal ecosystems related to linked democracy we should rely both on infrastructures, programs and artificial tools, *and* on the legal instruments and models to develop better and smart stakeholder governance. Responsive law is still an ideal. Linked democracy, as it has been presented in previous chapters, is a way to organise knowledge, institutions, and people to foster interoperability, remove silos, and create a secure framework for data sharing. We have already shown (ibid. 2017, Poblet et al. 2017) that it might operate to frame the connection between expert, collective, and personal knowledge in public health, allowing and empowering people to manage their own medical Electronic Health Records (EHRs) (also referred to as Medical Health Records [MHR]) in a safe and efficient way. However, as Robert Mathews has reminded in his introductory article for a *Health & Technology* special issue on privacy and medicine, "privacy desperately needs a common language, and a universal frame of reference, but it lacks for one" (Mathews 2017, 268). Well: the same is needed for the rule of law. We desperately need a *lingua franca*, a reliable meta-rule of law with a global scope, but we lack for one.

The distinction between *normative Semantic Web Regulatory Models* (nSWRM) and *institutional Semantic Web Regulatory Models* (iSWRM) (Casanovas 2015a, b) is relevant here. The former ones are based on semantic languages, encompassing almost exclusively inferential tools and RDF, RuleML SPARQL, OWL (among many other languages). In this sense, implementation is not a modelling priority. Digital Rights Management (DRM), Rights Expression Languages (REL), machine processable languages for the expression of licenses, such Open Digital Rights languages (ODRL) constitute privileged examples: the ODRL Core Model was

[60]See the recent surveys on business process regulatory compliance (Hashmi et al. 2018a), and on legal compliance (Casanovas et al. 2017c), Hashmi et al. (2018b) .

designed "to be independent from implementation" (2009).[61] But this is not the same for iSWRM. Conversely, they need to be much more attentive to the community of users and their organisations. iSWRM allow people to communicate, interact, share and set self-regulated collectives for specific purposes. They help to rebuild, maintain and change social bonds. Regulations applicable to platforms addressing e-learning, e-health, disaster management, crisis-mapping, or political participation are some examples. Terminologies (multi-lingual term banks), cotrolled vocabularies and content-related thesauri help implementing this institutional dimension of regulatory models (Rodríguez-Doncel et al. 2016).

However, this is not an absolute distinction, for institutions and norms are built alike and they often constitute distinctive sides of the same socio-legal ecosystem. Would it be possible to speak of *personal* ecosystems? For example, when I make a personal use of a Creative Commons license, should I be considered a member, element or component of the CC ecosystem? According to the organisation, there is an affirmative answer for this question:

> Initially we define the ecosystem as the network in which CC operates. Creative Commons often must respond to events over which we have little control or influence. These events arise from the fields of technology, society and non-users of CC licenses, and economic, regulatory and environmental influences. CC exerts some control and influence over licensing of digital content; users of CC licenses, our Affiliates and the digital commons, and the technical infrastructure we use. CC has a high degree of control over our internal processes, how we communicate and promote our work and our suppliers.[62]

This means equating ecosystems with the performance and scope of social networks. Our use of the term in a broad sense can also encompass this version, as this is referred to as the implementation of codes, rules and principles empowering the user and having an impact on her behaviour. It empowers the user to choose and select the framework she wants for labelling and managing her personal content on the web. But the regulation itself is not institutionally-driven. It does not create and manage the public identity for the user. The user does.

An institutionally-driven model instead focuses on the identity of the social group that creates or uses the tool as a sufficient condition to constitute the institution. It intends to mainly set up a structured environment for the community or social group that comes up as a result of its inception.

5.5 Conclusions and Future Work

In this chapter, (i) we have presented innovative forms of governance, (ii) advanced a set of minimal conditions for the rule of law on the web; (iii) introduced some of the requirements for legal interoperability, (iv) and proposed a conceptual scheme to frame socio-legal ecosystems.

[61]https://www.w3.org/2012/09/odrl/archive/odrl.net/2.0/DS-ODRL-Model-20090923.html.

[62]https://wiki.creativecommons.org/wiki/Research.

The thread that runs through the entire chapter is that the rule of law can work as the general and global framework that gets together some regulatory instruments that have commonly been kept disjointed—national, international and responsive law; policy, and better, smart and data governance; semantic web languages, and algorithmic governance.

The rule of law constitutes an ideal yet to be developed for the web of linked data. Let's be reminded of the W3C five-star principles for the web: (i) make your stuff available on the web under an open license; (ii) make it available as structured data; (iii) make it available in a non-proprietary open format; (iv) use URIs to denote things; (v) link your data to other data to provide context.[63]

The notion of linked democracy embraces them, but it should provide the adequate protections and incentives to foster them safely and appropriately. Berners-Lee blogged in 2009: "It's not the Social Network sites that are interesting —it is the Social Network itself. The Social Graph. The way I am connected, not the way my Web pages are connected." He called it the *Giant Global Graph*.

This is implicitly echoing the same problems encountered by political philosophers in the 16th and 17th centuries. It reminds another, less gentle, artificial giant. If we don't want to go back to the contractual notions of covenant, pact and delegation of power, we should be able to come up with some notions to empower and protect people and enhance their rights. The notions of *meta-rule of law* and sustainable *socio-legal ecosystems* point at the way *we* all should be connected. The link between the individuals and the collective.

The quadrant we have drawn (hard law, policy, ethics and soft law) can be used as a sort of regulatory quadrant for the sources of the rule of law. But this is an idealization: regulations at the implementation level are hybrid; they encompass norms, principles and values from all sections. Likewise, institutions connecting linked data with people, platforms and ecosystems can be built in many different ways. They set up a *hybrid* public space, between the market, the state and civil society—a *relational* notion of law, in which rights and duties can be assigned with different degree of compliance and enforcement.

The four notions of validity introduced in this chapter are related to legal governance. They can be used for different purposes. Positive validity is often assumed by semantic web developers as an ontological commitment. Formal validity refers to the internal consistency of models. Once established as a reasonable threshold (this would be a golden rule), composite validity can be used for evaluating the legal compliance of platforms focusing on their informational flows. This can be done independently of their aims and objectives—political crowdsourcing, crisis and disaster management, or security and open source intelligence. Ecological validity refers to the creation of legal linked data ecosystems by institutional means, i.e. through shared systemic (not just semantic) interoperability building. Compliance through Design (CtD) is one of the conceptual ways we can follow to set a reliable institutional framework.

---

[63] https://5stardata.info/en/.

CtD can be operationalised at different social, legal, and jurisdictional levels. For example, to enhance bottom-up participation (Karamagioli et al. 2017; Poblet 2018), or to link the rule of law to constitutional rights on specific national grounds. At that level, the ideas of open access and open constitutional courts (Keyzer 2010) are close to open rights and linked open data ecosystems. They can be readjusted to the dimensions of the next stages of the web illustrated in Figs. 5.2 and 5.3.

From a theoretical point of view, our conceptualization has two important political consequences. The first one is that within the web of data, 'legality' cannot be taken as the result of the activity of official representatives, the judiciary, government members and state agencies in a national state, *alone*. In a linked democracy model, legality comes from the grassroots as well, and it can be the result of the interaction of agents (all kind of agents: human and artificial, individual and collective) that respect the rule of law. It is a collaborative endeavour.

The meta-model has a second consequence. If these distinctions make any sense, it is not necessary to keep the sharp Weberian divide between *legitimacy* and *legality*; i.e. the strict separation between the ground of the political system (e.g. based on a majority rule) and its development through a legal autonomous system. Democracy and legality are intertwined. In this way, democracy is not deemed to be just a political form that shapes constitutions and laws, but a process to organise *innovative* and *shared* knowledge that empowers individuals, i.e. people, at a global level on the web.

References

Abbott KW, Snidal D (2000) Hard law and soft law in international governance. International Organization. Summer 54(3):421–456. https://doi.org/10.1162/002081800551280

Abel RL (2018) Law's wars: The fate of the rule of law in the US 'war on terror'. Cambridge University Press, UK

Aldewereld H, Boissier O, Dignum V, Noriega P, Padget JA (eds) (2016) Social coordination frameworks for social technical systems, LGTS, vol 30. Springer, Dordrecht. https://doi.org/10.1007/978-3-319-33570-4

Andrighetto G, Governatori G, Noriega P, van der Torre LW (2013) Normative multi-agent systems, vol 4. Schloss Dagstuhl-Leibniz-Zentrum für Informatik

Araszkiewicz M, Casanovas P (2016) On legal validity. In: Hoekstra R (ed) JURIX 2016, Legal knowledge and information systems, vol 294. IOS Press, Amsterdam, pp 125–130

Athan T, Governatori G, Palmirani M, Paschke A, Wyner AZ (2014) Legal interpretations in LegalRuleML. In: CEUR 1296, SW4LAW + DC@ JURIX

Athan T, Governatori G, Palmirani M, Paschke A, Wyner A (2015) LegalRuleML: Design principles and foundations. In: Faber W., Paschke A. (eds) Reasoning Web. Web Logic Rules. Reasoning Web 2015. Lecture notes in computer science, 9203:151–188. Springer, Cham

Ayres I, Braithwaite J (1995) Responsive regulation: transcending the deregulation debate. Oxford University Press

Bäckstrand K (2006) Democratizing global environmental governance? Stakeholder democracy after the World Summit on Sustainable Development. Eur J Int Relat 12(4):467–498. https://doi.org/10.1177/1354066106069321

Bhardwaj A, Singh W (2017 Dec) Systematic review of big data analytics in governance. In 2017 international conference on intelligent sustainable systems (ICISS). IEEE, pp 501–506

Balke T, da Costa Pereira C, Dignum F, Lorini E, Rotolo A, Vasconcelos W, Villata S (2013) Norms in MAS: definitions and related concepts. In: Dagstuhl follow-ups (4). Schloss Dagstuhl-Leibniz-Zentrum für Informatik

Bench-Capon TJM, Coenen FP (1992) Isomorphism and legal knowledge based systems. Artif Intell Law 1(1):65–86. https://doi.org/10.1007/BF00118479

Bench-Capon TJM, Gordon TF (2009) Isomorphism and argumentation. In: Proceedings ICAIL '09, ACM, New York, pp 1–20. https://doi.org/10.1145/1568234.1568237

Bexell M, Tallberg J, Uhlin A (2010) Democracy in global governance: the promises and pitfalls of transnational actors. Glob Gov 16(1):81–101. https://doi.org/10.4103/cs.cs_15_104

Bizer C, Heath T, Berners-Lee T (2011) Linked data: the story so far. In: Semantic services, interoperability and web applications: emerging concepts IGI Global, p. 2015-227

Boella G, van der Torre L, Verhagen H (2007) Normative multi-agent systems. In: Dagstuhl seminar proceedings 07122, Internationales Begegnungs- und Forschungszentrum für Informatik (IBFI), Schloss Dagstuhl, Germany

Boella G, Tosatto SC, Ghanavati S, Hulstijn J, Humphreys L, Muthuri R, Rifaut A, van der Torre L (2014) Integrating legal-URN and Eunomos: towards a comprehensive compliance management solution. In: Casanovas P et al (eds) AI approaches to the complexity of legal systems, AICOL 2013. LNCS 8929. Springer, Berlin, pp 130–144

Boer AWF (2009) Legal theory, sources of law and the semantic web. IOS Press, Amsterdam. https://doi.org/10.3233/978-1-60750-003-2-i

Braithwaite J (2017) Types of responsiveness. In: Drahos P (ed) Regulatory theory: foundations and applications. ANU Press, Canberra, pp 117–132

Brenton C (2017) CLOC: joining forces to drive transformation in legal: bringing together the legal ecosystem. In: Liquid Legal Springer, Cham, 2003–2010

Brous P, Janssen M, Vilminko-Heikkinen R (2016) Coordinating decision-making in data management activities: a systematic review of data governance principles. International conference on electronic government and the information systems perspective. Springer, Cham, pp 115–125

Carothers T (1998) The rule of law revival. Foreign Aff 77(2):95–106. https://doi.org/10.2307/20048791

Casanovas P, Casellas N, Vallbé JJ, Poblet M, Benjamins VR, Blázquez M, Peña R, Contreras J (2006) Semantic web: a legal case study. In: Davis J, Studer R, Warren P (ed) Semantic web technologies: trends and research. Ed. Wiley, Chichester, pp 259–280

Casanovas P (2012) A note on validity in law and regulatory systems. Quaderns de filosofia i ciència 42:29–40

Casanovas P (2013) Agreement and relational justice: a perspective from philosophy and sociology of law. In: Ossowski S (ed) Agreement technologies. Springer, Dordrecht, pp 17–41

Casanovas P (2017) Sub Lege Pugnamus. De la Gran Guerra a les Grans Dades. Publicacions de la Universitat de Barcelona, Barcelona

Casanovas P (2015a) Conceptualisation of rights and meta-rule of law for the web of data, Democracia Digital e Governo Eletrônico (Santa Caterina, Brazil) 12, 18–41; repr. J Gov Regul 4(4):118–129

Casanovas P (2015b). Semantic web regulatory models: why ethics matter. Philos Technol. Special Issue on Inform Soc Ethical Inq 28(1):33–35. https://doi.org/10.1007/s13347-014-0170-y

Casanovas P, Lauroba E, Magre J (2011) Introducción. In: Casanovas P, Lauroba E, Magre J (eds), Libro Blanco de la Mediación en Cataluña. Generalitat de Catalunya, Ed. Huygens, Barcelona, pp 173–178

Casanovas P, Oboler A (2018) Behavioural compliance and law enforcement in online hate and fear speech, TERECOM 2018, technologies for regulatory compliance. In: Proceedings of the 2nd workshop on technologies for regulatory compliance co-located with the 31st international conference on legal knowledge and information systems (JURIX 2018) Groningen, The Netherlands, pp 125–134. http://ceur-ws.org/Vol-2309/11.pdf

Casanovas P, Palmirani M, Pagallo U, Sartor G (2014a) Law, social intelligence, nMAS and the semantic web: an overview. In: Casanovas P et al (ed) AI approaches to the complexity of legal systems IV. Social intelligence, models and applications for law and justice systems in the semantic web and legal reasoning. LNAI 8929. Springer, Heidelberg, pp 1–10

Casanovas P, Arraiza J, Melero F, González-Conejero J, Molcho G, Cuadros M (2014b) Fighting Organised Crime through Open Source Strategies: Regulatory Strategies of the CAPER Project. Legal knowledge and information systems. In: Hoekstra R (ed) JURIX 2014: the twenty-seventh annual conference, Foundations on artificial intelligence n. 271, IOS Press, Amsterdam, pp 189–199

Casanovas P, Palmirani M, Peroni S, van Engers T, Vitali F (2016) Semantic web for the legal domain: the next step. Semantic Web 7(3):213–227. https://doi.org/10.3233/SW-160224

Casanovas P, Rodríguez-Doncel V, González-Conejero J (2017a) The role of pragmatics in the web of data. In: Capone A, Poggi F (eds) Pragmatics and law. Practical and theoretical perspectives. Springer, Dordrecht, Heidelberg, pp 293–330

Casanovas P, Mendelson D, Poblet M (2017b) A linked democracy approach for regulating public health data. Health Technol 7(4):519–537

Casanovas P, Gonzalez-Conejero J, de Koker L (2017c) Legal compliance by design (LCbD) and through design (LCtD): preliminary survey. In: TERECOM. Proceedings of the 1st workshop on technologies for regulatory compliance co-located with the 30th international conference on legal knowledge and information systems (JURIX 2017), CEUR 2049, pp 33–49

Casellas N, Bruce TR, Frug S, Bouwman S, Dias D, Lin J, Marathe S, Rai K, Singh A, Sinha D, Venkataraman S (2012) Linked legal data: improving access to regulations. In: Proceedings of the 13th annual international conference on digital government research (DGO 2012), ACM, New York, US, 2012, pp 280–281. https://doi.org/10.1145/2307729.2307785

Celino I, Corcho O, Hölker F, Simperl E (2018) Citizen science: design and engagement (Dagstuhl seminar 17272). In: Dagstuhl reports 7(7). Schloss Dagstuhl-Leibniz-Zentrum fuer Informatik

Cicourel AV (2007) A personal, retrospective view of ecological validity. Text Talk 27(5–6):735–752. https://doi.org/10.1515/TEXT.2007.033

Ciambra A, Casanovas P (2014) Drafting a composite indicator of validity for regulatory models and legal systems. In: Casanovas P, Palminari M, Pagallo U, Sartor G (eds) AI approaches to the complexity of legal systems IV. Social intelligence, models and applications for law and justice systems in the semantic web and legal reasoning, LNAI 8929, Springer, pp 70–82

Chen CP, Zhang CY (2014) Data-intensive applications, challenges, techniques and technologies: a survey on big data. Inf Sci 275:314–347

Cheesman N (2015) Opposing the rule of law. How Myanmar courts make law and order. Cambridge University Press

Christiaanse R, Ghose A, Noriega P, Singh MP (2014) Characterizing artificial socio-cognitive technical systems. In: Herzig A, Lorini E (eds) Proceedings of the European conference on social intelligence (ECSI-2014), Barcelona, Spain, 3–5 Nov 2014. CEUR workshop proceedings, 1283, pp 336–346

Christiaanse R, Hulstijn J (2012) Control automation to reduce costs of control. International conference on advanced information systems engineering. Springer, Berlin, pp 322–336

Clarke SGD, Stella G (2011) ISO 25964: a standard in support of KOS interoperability. In: Facets of knowledge organization: proceedings of the ISKO UK second biennial conference, 4–5 July 2011, London, pp 129–134

Colesky M, Ghanavati S (2016) Privacy shielding by design—a strategies case for near-compliance. In: Requirements engineering conference workshops (REW), IEEE International, pp 271–275

Corcho O, Poveda-Villalón M, Gómez-Pérez A (2015) Ontology engineering in the era of linked data. Bull Assoc Inform Sci Technol 41(4):13–17

Curtotti M, McCreath E, Bruce T, Frug S, Weibel W, Ceynowa N, Weibel W (2015) Machine learning for readability of legislative sentences. In: Proceedings of the 15th international conference on artificial intelligence and law, ACM, New York, pp 53–62

d'Aquin M, Motta E, Sabou M, Angeletou S, Gridinoc L, Lopez V, Guidi D (2008) toward a new generation of semantic web applications. IEEE Intell Syst 23(3):20–28. https://doi.org/10.1109/MIS.2008.54

d'Aspremont J, Besson S, Knuchel S (eds) (2017) The sources of International law: an introduction. In: The Oxford handbook of the sources of International law. Oxford University Press, Oxford, pp 1–39

Dignum V (2018) Ethics in artificial intelligence: introduction to the special issue. Ethics Inform Technol 20:1–3. https://doi.org/10.1007/s10676-018-9450-z

Drahos P (ed) (2017) Regulatory theory: foundations and applications. ANU Press, Canberra

Domingue J, d'Aquin M, Simperl E, Mikroyannidis A (2014) The web of data: bridging the skills gap. IEEE Intell Syst 29(1):70–74

D'Rosario M, Zeleznikow J (2018) Compliance with International soft law: is the adoption of soft law predictable? Int J Strateg Decis Sci (IJSDS) 9(3):1–15

Duong TH, Nguyen HQ, Jo GS (2017) Smart data: where the big data meets the semantics. Comput Intell Neurosci

Erlanger H, Garth B, Larson J, Mertz E, Nourse V, Wilkins D (2005) Is it time for a new legal realism. Wisconsin Law Rev 2:335–363

Floridi L (ed) (2015) The onlife manifesto. Being human in an hyper-connected era. Springer, Dordrecht

Fransen LW, Kolk A (2007) Global rule-setting for business: a critical analysis of multi-stakeholder standards. Organization 14(5):667–684. https://doi.org/10.1177/1350508407080305

Feigenbaum EA (1984) Knowledge engineering: the applied side of artificial intelligence (1982). Ann N Y Acad Sci 426:91–107

Francesconi E, Küster MW, Gratz P, Thelen S (2015) The ontology-based approach of the publications office of the EU for document accessibility and open data services. In: Kő A, Francesconi E (eds) International conference on electronic government and the information systems perspective, EGOVIS-2015. Springer, LNCS, Cham, pp 29–39

Garner JH, Hickman MJ, Malega RW, Maxwell CD (2018) Progress toward national estimates of police use of force. PLoS ONE 13(2):e0192932

Gel'man V (2004) The unrule of law in the making: the politics of informal institution building in Russia. Eur-Asia Stud 56(7):1021–1040

Ginsburg T, Tamir M (2008) Rule by law: the politics of courts in authoritarian regimes. Cambridge University Press, Cambridge

Gordon TF, Governatori G, Rotolo A (2009) Rules and norms: requirements for rule interchange languages in the legal domain. In: Governatori G, Hall J, Paschke A (eds) International workshop on rules and rule markup languages for the semantic web. LNCS 5858. Springer, Berlin, pp 282–296

Gottschalk P (2009) Maturity levels for interoperability in digital government. Gov Inform Q 26:75–81. https://doi.org/10.1016/j.giq.2008.03.003

Governatori G, Indulska M, Zu Muehlen M (2009) Formal models of business process compliance. JURIX, Rotterdam

Greenleaf G (2009) AustLII's business models: Constraints and opportunities in funding free access to law. In: Peruginelli G, Ragona M (eds) Free access, quality information, effectiveness of rights. Publishing Academic Press, Florence, Italy, pp 423–436

Greenleaf G, Mowbray A, Chung P (2013) The meaning of free access to legal information: a twenty year evolution. SSRN Electron J. https://doi.org/10.2139/ssrn.2158868

Grabowski A (2013) Juristic concept of the validity of statutory law. A critique of contemporary legal nonpositivism. Springer, Dordrecht

Gunderson L, Cosens B (2018) Case studies in adaptation and transformation of ecosystems, legal systems, and governance systems. In: Cosens B, Gunderson L (eds) Practical panarchy for adaptive water governance. Springer, Cham

Gunningham N, Grabosky P, Sinclair D (1998) Smart regulation: designing environmental policy. Oxford University Press, Oxford

Gunningham N, Sinclair D (2017) Smart regulation. In P. Drahos (ed) Regulatory theory. Foundations and applications, Canberra, ANU Press, pp 133–148

Hashmi M, Governatori G, Lam HP, Wynn MT (2018a) Are we done with business process compliance: state of the art and challenges ahead. Knowl Inf Syst 57(1):79–133

Hashmi M, Casanovas P, de Koker L (2018b) Legal compliance through design: preliminary results, TERECOM 2018. Technologies for regulatory compliance, In: Proceedings of the 2nd workshop on technologies for regulatory compliance co-located with the 31st international

conference on legal knowledge and information systems (JURIX 2018) Groningen, The Netherlands, pp 59–72. http://ceur-ws.org/Vol-2309/06.pdf
Hens L, Bhaskar N (2005) The world summit on sustainable development: the Johannesburg conference. Springer, Dordrecht
Hoekstra R (2009) Ontology representation design patterns and ontologies that make sense. IOS Press, Amsterdam
Hoekstra R (2010) The knowledge reengineering bottleneck. Semant Web 1(1, 2):111–115
Hutchins E (1995) Cognition in the wild. The MIT Press, Cambridge Mass.
Hutchins E (2006) The distributed cognition perspective on human interaction. In: Tomasello M, Enfield N, Levinson SC (eds) Roots of human sociality: culture, cognition and interaction 1. Berg Publishers, Oxford, pp 375–398
Hutchins E (2010) Cognitive ecology. Top Cogn Sci 2(4):705–715
Just N, Latzer M (2017) Governance by algorithms: reality construction by algorithmic selection on the Internet. Media Cult Soc 39(2):238–258. https://doi.org/10.1177/0163443716643157
Khan N, Yaqoob I, Hashem IAT, Inayat Z, Ali M, Kamaleldin W, Alam M, Shiraz M, Gani A (2014) Big data: survey, technologies, opportunities, and challenges. Sci World J
Karamagioli E, Karatza M, Xydia S, Gouscos D (2017) Participatory constitutional design: a grassroots experiment for (re) designing the constitution in Greece. In: Paulin A et al (eds) Beyond bureaucracy. Towards sustainable governance informatisation. Springer, Dordrecht, pp 151–166
Karlsson-Vinkhuyzen S, Vihma A (2009) Comparing the legitimacy and effectiveness of global hard and soft law: an analytical framework. Regul Gov 3:400–420
Keyzer P (2010) Open constitutional courts. The Federation Press, Annandale
Kirrane S, Villata S, d'Aquin M (2018) Privacy, security and policies: a review of problems and solutions with semantic web technologies. Semant Web 9:153–161. https://doi.org/10.3233/SW-180289
Koops BJ, Leenes R (2014) Privacy regulation cannot be hardcoded. A critical comment on the 'privacy by design' provision in data-protection law. Int Rev Law, Comput Technol 28(2):59–171
Koops BJ, Newell BC, Timan T, Skorvanek I, Chokrevski T, Galic M (2016) A typology of privacy. U Pa J Int L 38:483–575
Kun L, Beuscart R, Coatrieux G, Quantin C, Mathews R (2008) Improving outcomes with interoperable EHRs and secure global health information infrastructure. In: Bos L et al (eds) Medical and care compunetics 5. IOS Press, Amsterdam, pp 68–79
Lam HP, Hashmi M, Scofield B (2016) Enabling reasoning with LegalRuleML. International symposium on rules and rule markup languages for the semantic web. Springer, Heidelberg, pp 241–257
Li Y (2012) Theories in online information privacy research: a critical review and an integrated framework. Decis Support Syst 54(1):471–481. https://doi.org/10.1016/j.dss.2012.06.010
Van Lamsweerde A (2001) Goal-oriented requirements engineering: a guided tour. In: Requirements engineering, 2001. Fifth IEEE international symposium on requirements engineering. IEEE Comput Soc:249–261. https://doi.org/10.1109/isre.2001.948567
van Lamsweerde A (2009) Requirements engineering: from system goals to UML models to software, vol 10. Wiley, Chichester, UK
Macaulay S (2005) The new versus the old legal realism: things ain't what they used to be. Wisconsin Law Rev 2:365–403
Macdonald T (2008) Global stakeholder democracy: power and representation beyond liberal states. Oxford University Press
Macdonald K, Macdonald T (2017) Liquid authority and political legitimacy in transnational governance. Int Theor 9(2):329–351. https://doi.org/10.1017/S1752971916000300
Malcolm J (2008) Multi-stakeholder governance and the internet governance forum. Terminus Press, Perth
Malcolm J (2015) Criteria of meaningful stakeholder inclusion in internet governance. Internet Policy Rev 4(4). https://doi.org/10.14763/2015.4.391
Mathews R (2017) Interrogating 'privacy' in a world brimming with high political entanglements, surveillance interdependence & interconnections. Health Technol 7(4):265–324. https://doi.org/10.1007/s12553-017-0211-5

McAdams RH, Nadler J (2008) Coordinating in the shadow of the law: two contextualized tests of the focal point theory of legal compliance. Law Soc Rev 42(4):865–898

Merry SE (2017) What is the rule of law? Perspectives from Myanmar: commentary on opposing the rule of law: how myanmar's courts make law and order by nick cheesman. Hague J Rule Law 9(1):11–14. https://doi.org/10.1007/s40803-016-0041-y

Mondorf A, Wimmer MA (2016) Requirements for an architecture framework for Pan-European e-government services. In Scholl H et al (eds) Electronic government. EGOVIS 2016. LNCS 9820. Springer, Cham, pp 135–150

Motta E (2013) 25 years of knowledge acquisition. Int J Hum-Comput Stud Arch 71(2):131–134. https://doi.org/10.1016/j.ijhcs.2012.11.002

Miles TJ, Sunstein CR (2008) The new legal realism. Univ Chicago Law Rev 75(2):831–851

Mitleton-Kelly E, Papaefthimiou MC (2002) Co-evolution of diverse elements interacting within a social ecosystem. In: Henderson P (ed) Systems engineering for business process change: new directions. Springer, London, pp 253–273

Müller JP, Fischer K (2014) Application impact of multi-agent systems and technologies: a survey. In: Shehory O, Sturm A (eds) Agent-oriented software engineering. Springer, Berlin, pp 27–53

Mun E (2015) Negative compliance as an organizational response to legal pressures: the case of Japanese equal employment opportunity law. Soc Forces 94(4):1409–1437

Nonet P, Selznick P (1978) Law and society in transition: toward responsive law. Octagon Books, NY

Nourse V, Shaffer G (2009) Varieties of new legal realism: can a new world order prompt a new legal theory? Cornell L Rev 95:61–138

Noriega P, López de Toro C, Montero R, Pérez Martínez (2011) Anexo: Prototipo de un Sistema Genérico de Apoyo a la Mediación. In: Casanovas P, Lauroba E, Magre J (Dirs.) Libro Blanco de la Mediación en Cataluña. Generalitat de Catalunya, Ed. Huygens, Barcelona, pp 985–1008

Noriega P, Padget J, Verhagen H, d'Inverno M (2014) The challenge of artificial socio-cognitive systems. COIN@AAMAS 2014, Paris

Noriega P, Verhagen H, d'Inverno M, Padget J (2016) A manifesto for conscientious design of hybrid online social systems. Coordination, organizations, institutions, and norms in agent systems XII. Springer, Cham, pp 60–78

Pagallo U (2015) Good onlife governance: on law, spontaneous orders, and design. In: Floridi L (ed) The onlife manifesto. Springer, Cham, pp 161–177

Pagallo U, Palmirani M, Casanovas P, Sartor G, Villata S (eds) (2018) Introduction: legal and ethical dimensions of AI, NorMAS, and the web of data. In: AI approaches to the complexity of legal systems. AICOL international workshops 2015–2017: AICOL-VI@JURIX 2015, AICOL-VII@EKAW 2016, AICOL-VIII@JURIX 2016, AICOL-IX@ICAIL 2017, and AICOL-X@JURIX 2017, Revised selected papers. LNAI 10791. Springer, Cham, pp 1–20

Palmirani M, Paschke A, Athan T (2012) 1. Isomorphism. June 29th, oasis-open.org

Palombella G (2009) The rule of law beyond the state: failures, promises, and theory. Int J Const Law 7(3):442–467. https://doi.org/10.1093/icon/mop012

Palombella G (2010) The rule of law as and institutional ideal. In: Morlino L, Palombella G (eds) Rule of law and democracy: inquiries into internal and external issues, vol 115. Brill, London, pp 1–38

Pitt J, Bourazeri A, Nowak A, Roszczynska-Kurasinska M, Rychwalska A, Santiago IR, Sanchez ML, Florea M, Sanduleac M (2013) Transforming big data into collective awareness. Computer 46(6):40–45

Pitt J, Diaconescu A (2015, July) Structure and governance of communities for the digital society. In: Autonomic computing (ICAC), 2015 IEEE international conference on autonomic computing. IEEE, pp 279–284

Poblet M (2018) From open to crypto: horizontal, distributed, privacy-enhancing technologies for civic and political action. In: 25 world conference of political science, Brisbane, 21–24 July

Poblet M, Casanovas P, Plaza E (2017) Linked democracy: artificial intelligence for democratic innovation, LINKDEM, In: Proceedings of the Workshop on Linked Democracy: Artificial intelligence for democratic innovation co-located with the 26th International joint conference on artificial intelligence (IJCAI 2017). http://ceur-ws.org/Vol-1897/

Pollock R (2013) Forget big data, small data is the real revolution d open knowledge foundation blog. http://blog.okfn.org/2013/04/22/forget-big-datasmall-data-is-the-real-revolution/ (consultation: 22 Aug 2018)

Provan KG, Kenis P (2008) Modes of network governance: structure, management, and effectiveness. J Public Adm Res Theor 18:229–252

Purnhagen K (2015) Why do we need responsive regulation and behavioural research in EU internal market law? In K. Mathis (ed), European perspectives on behavioural law and economics, Cham, Springer, pp 51–69

Rhodes RA (2007) Understanding governance: ten years on. Organ Stud 28(8):1243–1264

Rodríguez-Doncel V, Santos C, Casanovas P, Gómez-Pérez A (2015) A linked term bank of copyright-related terms. JURIX 2015, Legal knowledge and information systems. IOS Press, Amsterdam, pp 91–100

Rodriguez-Doncel V, Santos C, Casanovas P, Gomez-Perez A (2016) Legal aspects of linked data —the European framework. Comput Law Secur Rev 32(6):799–813. https://doi.org/10.1016/j.clsr.2016.07.005

Sartor G (2009a) Understanding and applying legal concepts: an inquiry on inferential meaning. In: Hage JC, von der Pfordten D (eds) Concepts in law. Springer, Dordecht, pp 35–54

Sartor G (2009b) Legal concepts as inferential nodes and ontological categories. Artif Intell Law 17(3):217–251. https://doi.org/10.1007/s10506-009-9079-7

Schmitz P, Francesconi E, Batouche B, Dombrovschi B, Duy D, Landercy SP, Parisse V (2016) Linked open data and e-participation in the EU law-making process. In: Kö A, Francesconi E (eds) International conference on electronic government and the information systems perspective, EGOVIS-2016. Springer, Cham, pp 79–89

Schmitz P, Francesconi E, Landercy SP, Batouche B, Touly V (2017) A knowledge organization system for e-participation in law-making. In: Proceedings of the 16th edition of the international conference on artificial intelligence and law, ACM, pp 245–248

Schoop M, Moor AD, Dietz JL (2006) The pragmatic web: a manifesto. Commun ACM 49(5):75–76

Selznick P (2003) Law in context' revisited. J Law Soc 30(2):177–186. https://doi.org/10.1111/1467-6478.00252

Shadbolt N, Hampson R (2018) The digital ape: how to live (in peace) with smart machines. Scribe Publications, Melbourne and London

Shepard RN, Chipman S (1970) Second-order isomorphism of internal representations: shapes of states. Cogn Psychol 1:1–17. https://doi.org/10.1016/0010-0285(70)90002-2

Siddiqa A, Hashem IAT, Yaqoob I, Marjani M, Shamshirband S, Gani A, Nasaruddin F (2016) A survey of big data management: taxonomy and state-of-the-art. J Netw Comput Appl 71:151–166. https://doi.org/10.1016/j.jnca.2016.04.008

Sileno G (2016) Aligning law and action, Doctoral dissertation, Ph. D. thesis, University of Amsterdam

Sileno G, Boer A, van Engers TM (2014) On the interactional meaning of fundamental legal concepts. In: Sileno G, Boer A, van Engers TM (eds) Proceedings of the 27th international conference on legal knowledge and information systems (JURIX 2014). Front Artif Intell Appl, vol 271. IOS Press, Amsterdam, pp 39–48. https://doi.org/10.3233/978-1-61499-468-8-39

Sileno G, Boer A, van Engers T (2015) Commitments, expectations, affordances and susceptibilities: towards positional agent programming. In: Chen Q, Torroni P, Villata S, Hsu J, Omicini A (eds) PRIMA 2015: principles and practice of multi-agent systems: 18th international conference, Bertinoro, Italy, LNAI vol 9387. Springer, Cham, pp 687–696. https://doi.org/10.1007/978-3-319-25524-8_52

Sierra C (2004) Agent-mediated electronic commerce. Auton Agent Multi-Agent Syst 9(3):285–301. https://doi.org/10.1023/B:AGNT.0000038029.82331.c0

Simon HA (1969, 1984, 1986) The sciences of the artificial. The MIT Press

Singh MP (2002a) The pragmatic web. IEEE Internet Comput 3:4–5

Singh MP (2002b) The pragmatic web: preliminary thoughts. In: Proceedings of the NSF-OntoWeb workshop on database and information systems research for semantic web and enterprises, pp 82–90

Sivarajah U, Kamal MM, Irani Z, Weerakkody V (2017) Critical analysis of big data challenges and analytical methods. J Bus Res 70:263–286

Taylor S, Boniface M (2017) HUB4NGI:: D2. 1 NGI guide V1

Tamanaha BZ (2004) On the rule of law: history, politics, theory. Cambridge University Press

Tamanaha BZ (2009) A concise guide to the rule of law. In: Walker et al (eds) Florence workshop on the rule of law. Hart Publishing Company, St. John's Legal Studies Research Paper No. 07-0082

Tamanaha BZ (2011) The rule of law and legal pluralism in development. Hague J Rule Law 3 (1):1–17. https://doi.org/10.1017/S1876404511100019

Troullinou P, d'Aquin M, Tiddi I (2018) Re-coding black mirror chairs' welcome & organization. In: Companion of the the web conference 2018 on the web conference 2018. International World Wide Web Conferences Steering Committee, pp 1527–1528

TOGAF (2017) An introduction to the European interoperability reference architecture (EIRA©) v2.1.0

Taylor V (2017) Regulatory rule of law. In: Drahos P (ed) Regulatory theory: foundations and applications. ANU Press, Canberra, pp 393–413

Uildriks N (2010) Mexico's unrule of law: implementing human rights in police and judicial reform under democratization. Lexington Books, Lanham

Union European (2017) New European interoperability framework promoting seamless services and data flows for European public administrations. Publications Office of the European Union, Luxembourg. https://doi.org/10.2799/78681

Vallbé J, Casellas N (2014) What's the cost of e-access to legal information? a composite indicator. In: Doing business research conference: past, present, and future of business regulation, McDonough School of Business, Georgetown University, Washington, DC, 20–21 Feb

Vogt KA, Gordon JC, Wargo JP, Vogt DJ, Asbjornsen H, Palmiotto PA, Clark HJ, O'Hara JL, Keeton WS, Patel-Weynand T, Witten E (1997) Ecosystem concept: historical and present review of definitions and development of ecosystem ecology, ecosystem management, and its legal framework. In: Vogt KA et al (eds) Ecosystems. Springer, New York, pp 13–114

Wyner A, Governatori G (2013) A study on translating regulatory rules from natural language to defeasible logic. In: RuleML 2013: the 7th international web rule symposium, held 11–13 July 2013, in Seattle, Washington, USA

Xu LD, Xu EL, Li L (2018) Industry 4.0: state of the art and future trends. Int J Prod Res 56 (8):2941–2962. https://doi.org/10.3233/ip-140329

Zhao-Hong Y, Hui-Yu W, Bin Z, Zhi-He H, Wan-Lin L (2018, April) A literature review on the key technologies of processing big data. In: 2018 IEEE 3rd international conference on cloud computing and big data analysis (ICCCBDA). IEEE, pp 202–208

Zuiderwijk A, Janssen M, Davis C (2014) Innovation with open data: essential elements of open data ecosystems. Inform Polity 19(1, 2):17–33

Chapter 6
Conclusion

Communication technologies have permeated almost every aspect of modern life, shaping a densely connected society where information flows follow complex patterns on a worldwide scale. The World Wide Web created a global space of information, with its network of documents linked through hyperlinks. And a new network is woven, the Web of Data, with linked machine-readable data resources that enable new forms of computation and more solidly grounded knowledge.

Parliamentary debates, legislation, information on political parties or political programs are starting to be offered as linked data in rhizomatic structures, creating new opportunities for electronic government, electronic democracy or political deliberation. Nobody could foresee that individuals, corporations and government institutions alike would participate in a joint space of information establishing mutually beneficial relationships.

Chapter 1 has presented in detail the technologies enabling the Web of Data and has sketched practices of much interest for experts in political studies. The concept of democracy, which has remained relatively unaffected by this wave of changes, needs a revision and the idea of a Linked Democracy is an exploratory contribution.

Chapter 2 has reviewed deliberative and epistemic models of democracy and traced how some of their features are present in the current ecosystem of civic technologies. Building on both these models and empirical examples of participatory ecosystems we propose the concept of Linked Democracy as a basis to represent distributed, technology-supported, collective decision-making processes where data, information, and knowledge are connected and shared by citizens. Chapters 3 and 4 expand this concept by sketching a multilayered model and preliminary suggesting some core properties that we connect with Ostrom's design principles for the effective management of common-pool resources.

Chapter 5, finally, outlines the regulatory frameworks for linked democracy ecosystems that we denominate 'socio-legal ecosystems' and, on top of them, the concept of 'meta-rule of law'. The chapter distinguishes between hard law, governance, soft law and ethics. They are connected and constitute what we have called the "legal quadrant" for the rule of law.

M. Poblet et al., *Linked Democracy*, SpringerBriefs in Law,
https://doi.org/10.1007/978-3-030-13363-4_6

The Web of Data is any data available on the web in any form, such as raw data files, data exposed via API, or IoT streams. Linked data is a subset of the former set, i.e. it is an approach to publishing and sharing data on the web, following the five rules proposed by Tim Berners-Lee. We have contended that the protections and principles of the substantive rule of law can be represented into the languages of the Web of Data and embedded into compliance systems to generate trust and to define the global space as a public space.

The notion of linked democracy operates within this space in which corporations, companies, rulers, providers, consumers and citizens are using all kinds of linked-data repositories that cannot be treated as separate silos, as they are (or will be) linked through graph-driven mechanisms. The notion of relational law points at the allocation of behavioural expectations (assignment of rights and obligations) in terms of a shared technological framework in which computer systems and human-machine interfaces create an aggregated value fostering the connection between Web 2.0 and Web 3.0. Our goal has been to provide a conceptual roadmap that helps us to ground the theoretical foundations for a meso-level, institutional theory of democracy.

The Web of Data has transformed the way we access, produce, share, and reuse information, data, and knowledge. Most likely, further developments will come in successive waves of innovations in distributed technologies, machine learning, image and voice recognition, etc. These technologies will shape in new ways how we behave, interact, and make decisions as individuals, groups, and crowds. But as citizens of free societies we should retain our say in these processes. In the digital era, this can be done by augmenting, enriching, and diversifying the ways to participate and align our decisions. This book has started to explore this path.

Index

M. Poblet et al., *Linked Democracy*, SpringerBriefs in Law,
https://doi.org/10.1007/978-3-030-13363-4

www.ingramcontent.com/pod-product-compliance
Lightning Source LLC
LaVergne TN
LVHW082348200926
848481LV00012B/3492
* 9 7 8 1 0 1 3 2 7 2 7 2 1 *